Choosing a CRM Vendor

Best Practices, Pitfalls, and the Myth of the Turnkey Solution

Andrew Schultz

CGW
PUBLISHING

2011

Choosing a CRM Vendor

Best Practices, Pitfalls, and the Myth of the Turnkey Solution

First Edition September 2011

ISBN 978-1-9082930-7-7

Published by:

CGW Publishing
B 1502
PO Box 15113
Birmingham
B2 2NJ
United Kingdom

www.cgwpublishing.com

mail@cgwpublishing.com

Contents

Acknowledgments

I thank my Heavenly Father and Jesus Christ for giving me the intellect, education, experience, and opportunity to write this work. I acknowledge the hand They have in any accomplishment with my name attached to it.

I also acknowledge the following people for their contributions to my life that, in one way or another, impacted this book:

My wife, Camille, who has given me her support and enthusiastic encouragement throughout our marriage, and our children Sydney, Spencer, and Cordelia, for giving me a lovely reason to work hard (and for staying quiet long enough for me to hear myself think and write ☺).

My parents, George and Becky, from whom I learned to take pride in hard work.

My CRM mentor, Owen West, who sparked my excitement for the "rich fusion of technology and business" that is CRM.

And, finally, Christopher Greenaway, for his excellent help and guidance in publishing this book.

CRM: The Illusion and the Reality

This book is about CRM (Customer Relationship Management) software, those who sell it, and those who buy it. My aim in writing is to help you understand the proper approach to evaluating and choosing a CRM software vendor – a process which, as you'll quickly learn, is as much about the buyer as it is about the vendor.

Success in your relationship with a CRM vendor, just like any relationship, requires you to know who you are, what you stand for, what you hope to gain from the relationship, and what you're willing to give.

In more technical terms, we're going to talk about what you should bring to the table in a CRM evaluation, especially in terms of defined requirements, which grow out of a defined strategy for customer relationships.

In my experience, the most prevalent causes for CRM implementations failing to deliver the expected outcomes are that those outcomes are *ill-conceived, poorly defined, or based on an out of the box vision obtained from a vendor*. Or, believe it or not, sometimes the expected outcomes are non existent. Maybe you believe it, because this describes you, in which case, I don't mean to offend, but I hope you'll accept my offer to learn more from this book.

By *ill-conceived*, I mean that the expected outcomes are unrealistic, are not suited to the business of the company doing the implementation, or that they simply fail to comprehend the purpose and capabilities of CRM software. Sometimes, ill-conceived expectations result from a misunderstanding of how CRM software capabilities will map to the needs of your particular business or department.

By *poorly defined*, I mean that the expected outcomes lack the high level business understanding that make them measurable in an implementation. Too many CRM implementations jump immediately into a discussion of what fields we need on which screens, without first discussing what we hope to achieve with CRM. This may result from assigning a manager with a purely day to day operational view of the company or department as the CRM implementation project leader, or it may come from an unwillingness to invest the time and planning required to create well defined objectives and requirements.

So... the ability to keep track of account hierarchies with parent and child accounts with different addresses isn't a well defined outcome. It's definitely a great feature requirement on your evaluation plan, but its value is limited if it's not tied to a driver of business success. Reducing the time it takes to manage customer service requests by properly structuring account hierarchies for better searchability is better.

Of course, there are those of us who just got the idea that we needed CRM from a friend, an advertisement, a white paper, a department head, or a vice president. Maybe that describes you? Don't worry, you're anonymous; there's no finger pointing here.

If so, then you don't have an in depth knowledge of what to expect from CRM. Your next step, now that a desire for CRM has been defined, is to develop the requirements and objectives. Without these, your chances of having a successful implementation are... well, first tell me what the word "successful" means to you.

You get the point; defining expected outcomes is essential to choosing a CRM software vendor that can help you achieve those outcomes.

The Myth of the Turnkey Solution

Congratulations! Your interest in CRM software demonstrates your readiness to take your company to the next level. CRM is a turnkey solution designed to supercharge your business. The promises of CRM include more sales, a lower cost of sales, more effective marketing campaigns, and more loyal customers. With our solution, nothing can stand between you and the nebulous vision of success that you're convinced CRM can turn to reality. And you're in luck! Step right up! You can be up and running on CRM by the end of the day today.

Whoa! Wake up!! Avast, evil vendor! Let's take a step back from the vendor sales and marketing messages for a minute. Don't blame them, they're just doing what vendors do; trying to sell you their product by convincing you that you need it. The product's feature set will work, there's no problem there. How you use the features to improve your company's performance is up to you. They must assume that you've got that part covered, which you do, right?

The promises of CRM are attractive. Even after the dose of reality I gave you in the first section, did you feel a sense of euphoria slowly creeping over you as you read the unrealistic paragraph above? Was there a dreamy smile on your face as you finished it? If so, I've got work to do, because if your conception of CRM is anything like what I wrote above, you're dreaming, or you've been lied to. Perhaps both.

What I wrote in that paragraph is really not a sensible thing to believe, and yet so many people become aware of "CRM Software" as some sort of front office panacea that's going to solve all of the inefficiencies and failures they deal with day to day, and all they have to do is sign up - *and they believe it*.

These people end up choosing a CRM software vendor and moving forward with their eyes closed, only to wake up months later to the reality that nothing has changed or improved. And, unfortunately, their oblivious conclusion is that they must have chosen the wrong software vendor.

Better Business: There's Just Not an App for That

Why do people believe this myth? I can think of a few reasons. Human nature wants things to be easy, and it wants to follow the path of least resistance.

When faced with a need to improve something in a business, it's easy to think that the answer can be as easy as making a purchase. And, when faced with the reality that the purchase didn't solve the problems or create the desired change, human nature again takes the easy way out by assigning blame. That's easier than doing the work of reevaluating assumptions and accepting responsibility for acting without the proper consideration or due diligence.

In addition, many people have friends from other companies who successfully use CRM software. These friends may be end users who see the value that the CRM software has at their own companies, but have no understanding of the effort, planning, strategy, and investment the management put into its implementation and adoption. Or, they may have obtained the vision wholesale from a CRM vendor spreading the bogus message of effortless CRM success.

The message that I hope to convey to you in writing this book is that when you're talking about improving the front office operations of your business, there's not simply an app for that. There are applications that can help you drive change and improvement, but they are tools that can only be effective when plied by a person or team who is committed to make the changes happen and who accepts accountability for the effort.

The Road to Recovery

Not everyone is so hopelessly stuck in this unproductive myth of CRM software. I've met many people who have learned from their early CRM missteps and made more productive choices afterward.

One such person with whom I spoke recently, the owner of a $40M IT firm of about 100 people, had implemented several CRM systems in the past, and was in the process of trying again. His company had started with an application I had never heard of before and which I couldn't find in a web search when I tried to look it up. Despite its obscurity, they spent $80,000 on that product.

They started out trying to self implement with their own technical employees. When they saw that they were headed for trouble, they hired an implementation partner to take over, but it was too late.

Thirty days later, they threw the software out the window. Crippled, they made the choice to self implement Goldmine, which, in the long run, cost a similar amount of money and left them without a solution that met their needs. When I spoke to this person, his comment to me was "Andy, I don't want to make another hundred thousand dollar mistake."

He was doing many things right this time around. He had looked for a subject matter expert, commonly called a SME in the consulting world, without any vendor loyalties to help him evaluate the applications offered by the different vendors. Admittedly, people like that are hard to find, as the trenches in the CRM battlefield have been dug pretty deeply.

Most CRM consulting firms don't partner with more than one or two CRM vendors. Those that do are the Accentures of the world, firms with whom his engagement would have been mutually unbeneficial because of his company's size and budget.

Unable to find a SME to perform an evaluation, he went to work within his organization, doing what the SME would have done; asking for documented requirements from each group in the business that would use the software. He also considered the other existing applications his company was using and would continue to use in the foreseeable future, like their ERP[a] application, and his requirements for CRM to integrate with them.

_____

a   Enterprise Resource Planning. The suite of applications used to manage accounting, finance, supply chain, and other back office functions.

I met this business owner at the very end of his search. He ended up choosing a CRM vendor that was very vertically focused on his company's industry. That's a great thing to find, and it was probably a good choice.

But there were two problems in the reasons for his decision; problems that made me doubt his company's ability to use the application effectively, even if it was the right choice for the organization. The first is that he chose this vertical solution because he felt like it knew what his business required better than he did himself. "They have features I didn't even know I needed", he said.

The second problem was that his evaluation was very feature focused. Both in his search for a SME and in his utilization of the requirements documentation he collected from his employees, he was looking for the perfect vendor who could provide the list of features he had collected from the groups in his business, rather than grabbing his business by the horns and designing a strategy that could then be supported by a CRM application. He understood the need to apply the software to specific business needs, but there was still no strategy informing the requests made by the different areas of the business.

In other words, this business owner's list of features seemed to be generated by departmental business processes that hadn't been scrutinized to see how a CRM application could change and optimize the way they worked. Rather, it was an eclectic wish list compiled by department heads whose experience with CRM software was apparently limited. The requests from the different groups lacked the insight of an overall strategy that would connect the groups and unify their efforts into a coherent value chain.

The resulting evaluation was a simple feature comparison to make sure the vendor applicants could at least do the "must haves" on the list. Incidentally, the list itself wasn't completely relevant to CRM software, and it was certainly uninspired in its grasp of the realm of possibility that exists for a company implementing a CRM application.

A good SME could have perhaps helped him see the need to construct the strategy first. Then, rather than dwelling on features with no real connection to business value, the ensuing evaluation would have been focused on the vendor's ability to support this company's strategy. After all, the perfect solution can't exist without first having a clear vision of what should be improved in the business. This basic problem statement is a prerequisite to the existence of a *solution*. The orchestrated set of methods for addressing the problems is the strategy. The strategy implemented is the solution.

In other words, if he could have partnered with a SME, he could have set his sights on the perfect *solution* early, rather than focusing on finding the perfect vendor. And I'm going to reveal a secret here that will change your CRM life if you let it: *there's a good possibility that more than one CRM vendor's application could deliver that solution perfectly well.*

That is the insight I want to convey forcefully here in this introduction. I also want to clearly state that the vendor choice does matter. The point is that it's not the only or the most important element of success.

In the interest of full disclosure, I'll tell you that my company, like most others who work with CRM applications, has a relationship with a vendor. My company is a Microsoft partner, fully invested in the success of Microsoft's product, called Microsoft Dynamics® CRM. But we actually don't sell CRM; we leave that to our customers, who are other Microsoft partners who help companies implement CRM, or who have software products that integrate with or 'talk to' Dynamics CRM.

But vendor loyalties aside, everyone who has any investment in the CRM space stands to gain significantly from the education of the buying public. The purpose of this book is to provide you with that education, so you can avoid being an unfortunate member of the "I Hate CRM" movement, the group of vaguely disenchanted CRM customers who still don't understand that their chosen CRM application's failure to deliver the value they expected is largely their own fault — or that it's something that they could begin to turn around immediately with the right understanding and actions.

Also, I would like to point out that the story shared in this introduction is of a mid sized company in the IT industry. Your company may be larger or smaller and in a different industry entirely. In case this may lead you to believe that this work is written only for companies of that size or in that industry, I state clearly here that it's not. In fact, a later chapter will deal with the necessary considerations for companies of different sizes as they evaluate and implement a CRM strategy and application. What I write will also have no specific industry focus, but there is also a later chapter that discusses industry specific solutions and customizing a CRM application to meet industry specific needs.

Introducing the Book

I'm going to start our educational journey by relating the notable story of the meteoric rise and fall of the world's biggest CRM vendor, Siebel Systems, and what you can learn from it to help you with your CRM vendor search.

We'll proceed from that story to some practical details in "The Three Pillars of CRM", where we'll talk about some of the fundamental tenets of CRM, grouped under three main headings: Marketing, Sales, and Service. There's nothing new or groundbreaking in this chapter; it's purely for those who aren't familiar with the basic purposes of CRM.

If this is too basic for you, feel free to skip to "Finding a Solution: CRM is Not a Car. Don't Buy it Like it's a Car", where we'll start to discuss the right and wrong mindsets for approaching a CRM purchase.

"Choosing a Vendor: Flawed Decision Criteria", is where we'll begin to discuss evaluation criteria, beginning with the criteria that's most often used improperly, followed in the next two chapters by a description of more effective criteria.

Juggernaut Down

The Fall of the Biggest CRM Vendor in the World, and What We Can Learn From It

The Woeful History of Siebel CRM

Tom Siebel was hosting his company's second quarter conference call with financial analysts on a Wednesday in July, 2002, when he said something utterly uncharacteristic. "We don't really have a thorough analysis of the [sales] pipeline with us here today."[1] As Adam Lashinsky puts it, that statement was "a little like Yo-Yo Ma neglecting to pack his cello for an appearance with the philharmonic."

Tom Siebel was the co-founder and CEO of Siebel Systems, the best in breed provider of CRM software at the time, and for a very short time afterward. In analyst Joshua Greenbaum's words "the wheels were already falling off"[2] by October 2002, although one could argue that was true at this conference call. Siebel had long touted his CRM software's ability to help companies make marvelous improvements to their sales forecasting capabilities. And now, at his company's official analyst call, he didn't have a report on his pipeline.

Siebel was looking at the beginning of the end for his company, whether he know it or not. A former Oracle executive, and once their top salesman, he had left that company after failing to convince CEO Larry Ellison that the software he developed internally for sales could sell as an enterprise software product. In a strange, somewhat cannibalistic turn of events, Siebel started Siebel Systems in 1993, enjoyed several years of almost unheard of success, and then, with the company reeling from the downturn following the .com bust and increased competition in the CRM space, sold Siebel Systems to his former nay-saying boss Larry Ellison and Oracle for $5.85 billion. I imagine Ellison wished he had just funded Siebel's proposal when Siebel still worked at Oracle.

What happened to Siebel Systems? I think their story is worth retelling here, simply because they were the original enterprise CRM player. Their struggles are the struggles that have plagued CRM as a whole for much of its lifetime, and there's a subtext relating to the satisfaction of Siebel customers that has a bearing on our discussion of relationships between CRM vendors and customers.

The terms "On Demand" "SaaS" "Software as a Service", and "Cloud" are used interchangeably in this chapter.

What's Siebel?

If you're a member of Generation Y (as I am – albeit a senior member, born at the end of 1979), whether or not you've ever even heard of Siebel Systems probably depends upon your career path.

If you're not in technology, or in the front office at an enterprise company where you have to use Siebel CRM, it's possible you may never have heard the name. But in the late 90's and early 2000's, Siebel was a brand on fire.

In 1999, the company was identified by Fortune Magazine as the fastest growing company in the United States. Its annual revenue between the years of 1995 and 1999 was $8M, $39M, $120M, $391.5M, and $790.9M, respectively. In 2000, revenue surpassed the billion dollar threshold.[3]

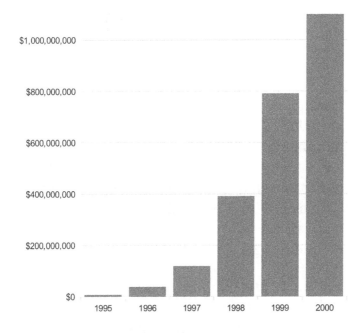

Not bad. $8M to over $1B in five years. Near its peak, Siebel held a 45% market share of the CRM market.[4]

What Happened to Siebel

In part, the .com bust and the bearish economy that followed caused Siebel to go through difficult times that precipitated its fire sale; but that would only be part of the story. Siebel was actually posting encouraging numbers in some categories; in January 2005, just months before its acquisition, *Information Week* ran a story with the optimistic title "Siebel's 2004 Even Stronger Than Expected."[5]

Tom Siebel had removed himself as CEO in 2004 amid floundering performance, passing the mantle to Mike Lawrie, a former SVP and 26 year employee of IBM. Even though some indicators began pointing in the right direction during his tenure, Lawrie's run as CEO lasted less than a year; on April 13, 2005, he was ousted, and George Shaheen, a member of the Board of Directors, assumed command. George Shaheen presided for roughly six months before Oracle acquired the company.

Despite the increased revenue, which continued in 2005 before the company's sale, more telling financial metrics conveyed the truth that the company was sinking:

"The company's second quarter figures this year put the final nail in the coffin. Sales were up from $301.1m to $313.6m as a result of improved maintenance, but license revenue, the real arbiter of performance, fell 17.4%."[6]

Apart from financials, some very important factors in Siebel's struggles are things that still play an important role in the CRM market today, as we have already discussed:

1. Customer satisfaction

2. The 'Cloud'

3. Integration with a company's existing 'stack' or infrastructure

Customer Satisfaction

We'll start with this one because it has the most drama. The drama has a point though. There were controversies surrounding Siebel's customer satisfaction rates, and at the end of the day, it turned out that the vendor was sending some inaccurate messages. The takeaway for us? Don't believe everything the vendor says.

I said this in the introduction to this book, and if you don't believe me, take a look.

In May 2002, a somewhat controversial analyst named Joshua Greenbaum wrote the following on his internet.com blog:

> In an industry not known for promoting the shy, quiet types, Tom Siebel stands out. His arrogance and self-assurance have made him the No. 1 software executive people love to hate. His partners live in fear and loathing, his competitors become apoplectic at the mention of his name, and analysts and the press are unanimous in their frustration at the company's closed-door, no-access-is-good policy.
>
> Ironically, the only people who seem to love Siebel are his customers -- of course, you have to take Tom's word on that. At every quarterly call, Tom claims his customer satisfaction ratings are in the stratosphere. Last fall he claimed a 96% approval rating from his customers (identical, incidentally, to his self-reported satisfaction rating from his employees). This winter customer satisfaction was at 95% and this spring it was "the highest it has ever been in the company's history." [7]

Greenbaum's incredulity regarding Siebel's customer satisfaction rating leads into insinuations that the company's culture in general is too close with its information to be trusted, and he provocatively mentions Enron and other less remembered corporate accounting scandals.

Greenbaum's article was sufficiently inflammatory to elicit a response from Stacey Wueste, Senior Director of Public Relations at Siebel, in which she retaliated with personal attacks on Greenbaum's journalistic credentials: "During particularly busy times, calls may not be immediately returned to people with whom we are not familiar or who lack a certain level of stature in the IT industry. I am sure that Mr. Greenbaum understands the need for prioritized communications."

Wueste repudiates Greenbaum's claims of secrecy, arguing that "Siebel Systems is recognized throughout the industry for the clarity, transparency, and quality of its financial disclosures", and that "our public disclosures are among the most accurate and comprehensive in the world." Wueste ends by addressing Siebel's customer satisfaction numbers, emphasizing that they are generated by a third party survey firm called Satmetrix. She smugly concludes that "Satmetrix also conducts similar research for other major corporations in the IT industry, and Siebel

Systems regularly receives the highest scores. The results speak for themselves."

Of course, it's hard to decide who to believe when both are arguing from extreme positions on opposite ends of the spectrum, with Greenbaum comparing Siebel to Enron and Wueste speaking in such glowing terms about world-class clarity and transparency. But, as others besides Greenbaum have noted, a 95% customer satisfaction score simply doesn't exist in the IT industry. People had a hard time believing those numbers, even decorated as they were with such effusive hyperbole as Wueste used here.

Lashinsky's 2002 *Fortune* article pointed out a problem with the Satmetrix customer satisfaction surveys: "What Siebel neglected to point out is that it is a minority investor in Satmetrix, and that Siebel board member James Gaither is also on the Satmetrix board."

That same month, Alorie Gilbert's *cnet* article noted the relationship, saying that "Siebel holds an equity stake in the firm [Satmetrix]" and discusses a customer satisfaction review of Siebel customers not commissioned by Siebel that returned contrasting results. The survey of twenty four Siebel customers conducted by Nucleus Research reported that more than half of them did not see a positive return on their Siebel CRM investment.

Gilbert quotes a representative from Nucleus Research who notes that each of the customers surveyed were success stories featured on Siebel's website, and then asks "If their success stories are having a difficult experience, what does that tell you about the broader population of Siebel customers?"

Indeed, several years later, new CEO Mike Lawrie declared "We need to be easier to work with... We need to be a better partner", apparently referring to the dismal percentage of customers, 41%, who said that their Siebel deployments had failed to meet expectations.[8] By this time, the illusions of 95% satisfaction had been officially shattered. So it appears that, in this instance, the nay-sayers were right about Siebel's own relationships with its customers.

When asked to explain the ironic lack of strong customer relationships for the Customer Relationship Management vendor, Mike Lawrie made the following statement, which contains insight very relevant to our discussion in this book:

> You are now dealing with portions of the employee population [CRM users in the front office, like sales, marketing, and service,] that have very different, nonlinear tasks that they do. So it becomes a much more difficult integration project, and in many ways, re-

engineering the front office is what helps companies transform their cultures. And transforming cultures is probably the most difficult task you can take on.

Those that are successful have a disproportionate share of benefits because it is a huge competitive differentiator. So it's the same old story. If you put in the time, you put in the effort, you do the work and do the planning, you get the results. If you don't do the aforementioned, you get less than outstanding results. Where we're refocusing the company on is how we can get more and more of our customers to get those outstanding results.[9]

This statement, in my experience, is spot on. According to its CEO, the fact that CRM took effort to implement properly was one of the major problems faced by a vendor who once ruled the CRM world. And, despite the titanic leaps ahead that CRM software has made over the intervening years since this statement was made, it's still true today. Realizing success with CRM takes planning and work.

But, of course, it's very uncommon for a vendor to communicate this, especially through marketing and sales messages. If the marketing and sales departments at Siebel were in the habit of communicating with the same swank magniloquence as Stacey Wueste from PR, then I have to say, I think they had created the "unmet expectations" problem for themselves.

Let's analyze the language Mike Lawrie is using to understand his position here. He's still using words like "outstanding results." Despite his admission that his company has a problem with customer satisfaction, he's still focused on communicating to the public, to YOU, as a CRM buyer, the "outstanding results" achieved by those rare customers who understood the work and planning required. Mr. Lawrie also says he's dedicated to getting more of Siebel's customers to that point, which would inevitably involve more work on the customers' part. Commendable, truly, but answer me this: do you think that communication about the "more work" part happens *before* or *after* you buy Siebel CRM?

To summarize, I'm saying that not much has changed in terms of what it takes to successfully implement CRM, or in what the vendors will tell you about it. Of course, today, the technical work is often much more streamlined, but the work of "re-engineering the front office" and "transforming cultures" is the same, and that's the part I'm emphasizing in this book.

"Siebel was once seen as a holdout among providers shifting to on demand software delivery."[10]

With the benefit of hindsight, that statement speaks volumes about Siebel's competitive disadvantage. Salesforce.com was a precocious newcomer to the CRM market in Siebel's heyday. In the early years, the larger software companies overlooked the threat from the cloud based CRM vendor. Near the end, however, short months before Siebel's surrender, analysts looking for a bright spot in another quarter of poor results from Siebel found it in the fact that the company had almost doubled the sales of its Siebel CRM OnDemand offering from the quarter before.

A week after George Shaheen assumed the top leadership position at Siebel from Mike Lawrie, less than six months before the company's sale was announced, Jim Wagner reported:

> Siebel's OnDemand strategy, which emerged only after companies like Salesforce.com proved there was such a big demand for

hosted CRM, has developed slowly, but officials are trying to make up for lost time.

It's an area they've handled well, [the CEO of a company that develops an add on application to Siebel CRM] said, despite his initial doubts about whether Siebel was entering hosted CRM wholeheartedly or as a wedge against Salesforce.com's growing popularity. He points to the sales compensation components added to Siebel's SMB program last year.

'When you're paying your sales teams to be aggressive in selling the OnDemand solution as part of your core component, that changes a lot', [the CEO] said. "I do believe they're out aggressively working this, not just upgrades for existing Siebel clients, but they are winning deals with their [OnDemand] solution with companies with no other Siebel relationship in place."[11]

Another report, referencing George Shaheen's statements from the same time period, says that "when freshly appointed Siebel Chief Executive George Shaheen first spoke to the customer relationship management (CRM) software maker's customers in April, he openly admitted that the company 'took its eye off the ball' in letting rivals such as Salesforce.com steal away clients with hosted applications services. At that event, and several times since, Shaheen has labeled Siebel's own hosted offering as one of its best chances for luring back customers and growing the company's software revenue."[12]

Since he had only recently become CEO when he made the statement, Shaheen would have been referring to poor decisions made in Mike Lawrie's era, or even in Tom Siebel's.

Less than a year earlier, in his already quoted interview with Mike Lawrie shortly after Lawrie's instatement as CEO, Alorie Gilbert asked "I couldn't help but notice that on the slides, you used in your keynote that OnDemand was in a smaller bubble than the bubbles representing business units, including traditionally packaged software and custom developed software. Are there some situations where subscription software doesn't make sense?" Lawrie's answer didn't demonstrate any commitment to further pursuance of that market.

Siebel did indeed experience encouraging growth in its On Demand offering, but its numbers were probably due to the fact that the market for On Demand software was quickly expanding, as well as the fact that it was "on the leading edge of a growth curve" which was fueled by pent up demand, but which wasn't likely to continue at the same rate, according to Jim Wagner's article.

This recognition of the importance of the Cloud was happening in 2005, several years before most of the population understood the difference between on-premise and Cloud software, and certainly several years before the term "Cloud" had any meaning.

Since then, the global recession that began to develop in 2007, as well as other influences, has super charged the expansion of the Cloud model of software application delivery. Now everyone who has even a marginal investment in understanding how software works knows the difference between applications that run locally or on-premise and those hosted in the Cloud.

Imagine how much more important this consideration is today, as you evaluate CRM applications, than it was in 2005, when it played a visible, recognizable role in the downfall of the world's largest CRM vendor.

Integration with a Company's Existing Stack

"Stack" is a slang term for the software a company uses to run its business, possibly derived from the way servers are stacked on top of each other in server racks, or from the way that sets of applications are built on top of each other. Modern companies have a very substantial investment in software, especially in "essential" business applications. This is a category which, for many, does not include CRM. Seeing CRM as non essential was probably even more common in Siebel's day, when CRM was still a relatively new application and concept.

A list of essentials often includes applications like:

- ERP for accounting, finance, supply chain and HR applications

- Email servers

- Core infrastructure like operating systems

- End user productivity tools like MS Office

Applications that aren't considered essential can increase their own real or perceived value by integrating with these existing applications, thus helping the customer leverage their existing software investments. An easy example of this is a CRM system that can show its sales users a history of orders and payments for a customer account, which is data that would typically reside in the ERP application; especially the payment history.

Another example of CRM-ERP integration would be allowing a salesperson to see current inventory levels for the products he sells inside of his CRM system. Software exists to give people better access to information, to streamline the flow of information through an organization.

A CRM application that sits like an island in an organization, disconnected from all of the other applications that hold critical business information, isn't nearly as attractive as one that can speak to these applications and contribute to the connectedness of the business.

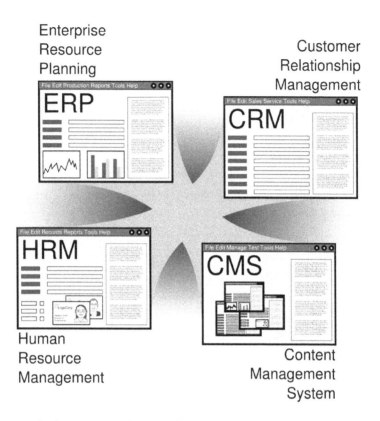

Enterprise Resource Planning

Customer Relationship Management

Human Resource Management

Content Management System

Siebel apparently tried to market its ability to connect to other applications, but at the time of their demise, Jason Stamper quotes Tom Siebel admitting that '"What really brought this together was a shift in market dynamics we've seen in the past three, four or five years.' He argued that businesses used to want to buy best of breed software from best of breed vendors, but now they want to buy integrated applications suites from fewer vendors: 'An integrated family of applications that minimize their cost structure' as he put it."[13]

The context of those "past three, four, or five years" Siebel mentions was the recession following the burst of the .com bubble, a time in which companies throttled their previously unrestrained spending because of tightened purse strings and bleak revenue forecasts. Sound familiar?

As I write this book in 2011, the current state of technology has been profoundly impacted by the recession that followed the bursting housing bubble in 2008, this time in the development of the Cloud and its radical departure from the immediately preceding models of delivering and monetizing technology. What changed, Tom Siebel is saying, is the way that companies thought about the value provided by software.

Competitors had been making this criticism of Siebel for some time. These quotes were uttered almost three years earlier:

Says Larry Ellison at Oracle, which markets a CRM application as part of its software suite: "The specialty vendors will die over time. I think Siebel falls into [that] category. The suites always win."

Craig Conway, CEO of PeopleSoft and, like Siebel, an Oracle veteran, adds "The CRM industry has changed. Now not only should CRM not be viewed as the center of the universe, but I question whether it's a separate category at all."[a]

Siebel became increasingly vulnerable to competitors from the ERP or HR software spaces who could leverage their existing base of customers to sell new CRM offerings that integrated with the other products their customers already owned. Fortune's Adam Lashinsky reported that "Though Siebel dominates CRM today, other players have an even bigger presence in the corporate world. SAP, which specializes in software that ties together back office operations of large companies, has 18,000 customers and is now trying to crack the CRM market. 'Our key is our installed base,' says Michael Park, SAP's vice president for global marketing. Siebel, by contrast, has about 3,500 customers."[b]

---

a   Lashinsky, Adam. Ibid.

b   Lashinsky, Adam. Ibid.

Conclusion

I share the story of Siebel because of its relevance to your choice of a CRM vendor today. I hope that this story will humanize your search for a vendor, and help you realize that name and reputation, while important, aren't the most important factors in your choice. CRM vendors are just companies like yours, and they are good at some things and poor at others, and they are susceptible to market trends and economic disturbances; some more than others. Your vendor selection criteria should include the strength of the company and its commitment to the CRM market.

Each of the three factors I highlighted in Siebel's downfall are also relevant to your choice. It's important that you understand your vendor's track record with customers realizing the promised value from their CRM investment, because you're going to be one of them. If you think you're special or different from other customers, you need to have a good reason to do so. Otherwise, you'll want to go with a vendor who has solid reference customers of a similar size and industry position as yourself. And remember Siebel's dissimulation, and don't trust everything the vendor tells you about their company or their track record.

It's very important that you understand the deployment options for the vendor's CRM application on your company's own servers or in the cloud. We'll discuss this more in depth in the chapter entitled "Choosing a Vendor: Appropriate Decision Criteria", but I hope I've demonstrated how important this consideration is for the CRM market.

There's no reason for a company purchasing CRM today to be limited to one option for the deployment model. This is especially true if that one option is on-premise, but it's also true for vendors whose only offering is in the cloud. You may decide to switch from one deployment type to another, for unforeseeable reasons, sometime down the road. It would be nice if you could do so with the least amount of effort.

Finally, it's important that you consider how the CRM application will integrate with your existing 'stack' or software infrastructure. Hopefully, the section in this chapter on that subject sufficiently elucidated the value of this capability. You may not intend to create any integrations between CRM and the applications from other areas of your business right now, but that certainly doesn't mean that this consideration should be taken off your list.

As you deploy your CRM application of choice, users will make requests for data from other systems, and the value in creating connections to those systems will increase the more entrenched your CRM solution becomes inside of your company. If you haven't carefully planned for this need, you may find yourself picking up this book and starting over again.

The Three
Pillars of CRM

The Three Pillars

CRM's big initial push was in the sales department. It became known by the moniker Sales Force Automation (SFA). That term is still used today to describe one of the main functions of CRM, but it's expanded to be a solution for the entire "front office", the part of a company that faces the customers.

The other two main functional categories are Marketing Automation and Service Automation. I know what you're thinking, and I agree; why is everyone's last name "Automation?" I'm suspecting nepotism.

The value that CRM can add to an organization is by no means limited to these three categories; we'll discuss how CRM can be customized to expand into other parts of the business in the "Advanced Vendor Considerations" chapter.

In this chapter, we're going to discuss each of these three "pillars" of core functionality.

CRM for Sales (Sales Force Automation)

So what results, exactly, is your sales team expecting from a CRM application? Since this book isn't an implementation guide, I'm going to talk high level about functionality that usually participates in a CRM solution for sales. You should understand that there's much more to talk about here, so the following will give you some ideas on things to look for and evaluate when choosing a vendor.

They key concept with SFA is using greater informational access to empower, organize, and, when possible, automate sales tasks to give your people more time on the street. These tasks could include reporting interactions with accounts, writing quotes or orders, getting approvals, and reporting pipeline data.

It's all about transitioning the old school sales guy with a stack of business cards, a killer instinct and a winning smile into an efficient force that can deliver more consistently and intelligently, and helping him collaborate with others in the company more regularly and effectively.

It's not about down playing or replacing the skills that were important to sales in those days gone by, it's about supporting those people who have those skills with a framework that will provide the organizational and teamwork elements that they often lack in their own personal skill set.

Lead Management

One way you can make your sales people more efficient is by giving them an organized set of leads and a system that tracks them. In the chaos of a salesperson's day, a lead delivered via email, on a napkin, a sticky note, an Excel sheet, or an in person conversation has a great chance of getting lost.

A lead assigned properly in a CRM application will stay on his list until he does something with it.

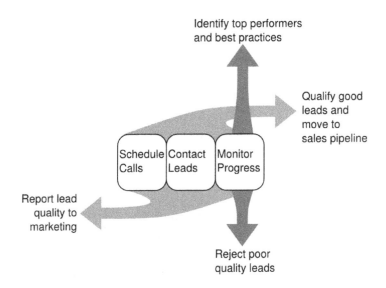

Identify top performers and best practices

Qualify good leads and move to sales pipeline

Schedule Calls | Contact Leads | Monitor Progress

Report lead quality to marketing

Reject poor quality leads

The beauty of lead management is the ability it gives the sales manager to ensure that proper follow through is occurring when leads are given to sales people.

Many sales people will only call a lead once or twice, and give up when they can't be reached or if the initial conversation isn't stellar. Research shows that it actually takes much more contact than that to properly qualify a lead, and a CRM application allows a sales manager to monitor and direct that contact.

We won't launch a discussion about lead quality here, but if poor lead quality is an issue with your company, a CRM application is a great place to gather specifics and start the conversation about improving the leads.

Sales Process and Opportunity Management

The second piece of a good SFA application is the next logical step in a sales process: the opportunity.

An opportunity represents a potential sale. At its most basic level, it's a record with an estimated revenue, a potential client, and an estimated close date. In the real world, there is typically much more information on the opportunity, including the stage it's currently at in the sales process.

That stage, if updated properly by the sales reps, generates the pipeline report that we'll discuss in the next section. If your sales process is complex or constrained by tasks that must be completed for an opportunity to advance from one stage to the next, it's often helpful to build a work flow that can automate some of those tasks, such as receiving approval from a department head for a price discount, scheduling an internal review, or something of that nature.

When an opportunity is closed, it is marked as won or lost. This gives a rep and the management a history of wins and losses, and can also track how many deals are being lost to competitors and why.

This information helps the management and executive team understand shifts that may be occurring in their competitive landscape.

Reporting, Dashboards and Analytics

"Dashboard" is kind of a buzzword among sales people, although it's becoming somewhat old hat from a CRM technology standpoint. A dashboard is a screen that shows multiple pieces of data in one glance, usually through a combination of charts, graphs, and tables. A good dashboard will have the capability to let the user "drill down" into the data, seeing greater and greater detail as he does so, until he arrives at the base record. In the case of this discussion, that would be a single opportunity.

For example, consider the following chart.

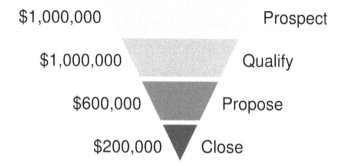

$1,000,000	Prospect
$1,000,000	Qualify
$600,000	Propose
$200,000	Close

Seeing the information this way would help a sales manager or executive understand if there's a need to initiate improvements, and where.

I should be able to click on one of the areas of the chart and see the data in greater detail. For example, perhaps I want to look at those records in the "Close" sales stage, by clicking on the blue part of the graph, I should be able to see those opportunities or a more specific graph, perhaps one that shows me the value of the opportunities in that stage grouped by their owners.

I say that the dashboard is becoming old hat because of the emerging capability to explore data in a more fluid, flexible manner. The dashboard is static; it's built to show a certain piece of information, and it shows it. A good CRM application will also allow a user to query the data easily and find out the answers to questions he has about it, similar to what I've described above.

CRM for Marketing
(Marketing Automation)

Marketing departments have a complicated job, when you think about it. The salesperson has a list of leads or accounts, and he goes and tries to sell to each one. It's not an easy job, but it's not one that usually causes the circuits to short out upstairs. Marketing, however, has the more complex task of managing multiple lists of leads and contacts, communicating with those lists multiple times in multiple ways, regarding multiple products and multiple offers. The mismanagement of this information leads to disgruntled customers who feel like they're getting spammed, who feel that the company doesn't know who they are or what they purchased, or who don't get the messages that could lead to their further purchase of the company's products.

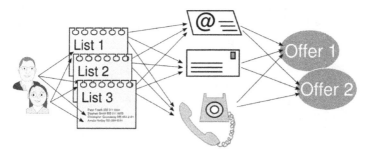

Certainly, the job of a marketer has changed a lot in recent years. Arguably, it has changed more than the jobs of those in the other two departments we're discussing in this chapter. It will continue to change dramatically in the near future as social media becomes increasingly entrenched as a means of communication. The functionality of a CRM application will need to adapt to this change. That being said, we're going to discuss some of the traditional functionality here, and maybe some of it will stay relevant through the rapid change in the next few years ahead.

Marketing Lists

This is step one for a marketer. Pretend a company has never done any marketing, and then they hire a marketing person. That person goes in on his first day, sits down at his desk, and writes this on a piece of paper:

First Item of Business:
Get a List

Without a list, the marketer doesn't have a job. With companies in certain industries, he may manage advertisements, it's true, but the days of the one to many blast advertisement have gone the way of the dinosaur for most companies, and are becoming increasingly ineffective.

But even in those companies who still run massive advertisements, your marketing people are going to want to work with lists of real people who they can communicate with regarding your company's products. These people may be contacts at companies who have purchased your products, people your employees have met at trade shows or events, or they could even be contacts purchased from a list vendor.

I worked with a health care network recently who had three types of people they needed to communicate with; elderly consumers of health care services or their family members, vendors of health care services or products, and health care professionals. They had the contact info for thousands of these types of people, all in one list.

When they sent out a communication to the list, it went to everyone. They weren't able to send consumer focused communications to the elderly and their families, or to send vendor focused communications to the vendors. Their motivation for implementing a CRM system was to obtain this capability.

A marketing list in CRM is a static or dynamic list of leads or contacts who all share certain characteristics. The definition of those characteristics is up to your marketing department and their marketing strategy, but some common ones are industry, company size, and products purchased in the past. If you're a B2C company, the same concept applies, but the company information such as size, industry, etc. are replaced by demographic information.

Campaigns

To communicate with the people in the marketing lists, the marketer will typically conduct a campaign. The campaign represents a specific set of communications to be sent to the people on the list, or the general public, regarding a certain offering or set of offerings.

The purpose of gathering these communications under the umbrella of a campaign is to achieve the following:

1. Keep track of the tasks that need to be completed internally to launch the campaign

2. Organize and plan the communications

3. Keep track of the money spent on this set of communications

4. Keep track of the response to this set of communications

There's a lot of value in simply grouping a set of communications under a campaign and keeping track of these few things, especially items three and 4. Doing so allows the marketers to obtain the following metrics on a campaign:

1. Return on Investment (ROI): When the campaign responses are tracked through the sales process, the revenue from those sales can be compared to the cost of the campaign (#3 above). This may be available in a standard report in the CRM application.

2. Cost per Response: Comparing the cost of the campaign to the number of responses helps the marketers understand the channels, techniques, and offers that can engage customers most inexpensively. Of course, that metric alone can be misleading

if it's not understood in conjunction with ROI as well.

3. Unique Metrics: Marketers can potentially obtain a host of other similar metrics that may be very valuable to your company, such as which types of communications and offers generate the responses that turn into sales most quickly, which ones generate the most responses, which ones work best at certain times of year, etc.

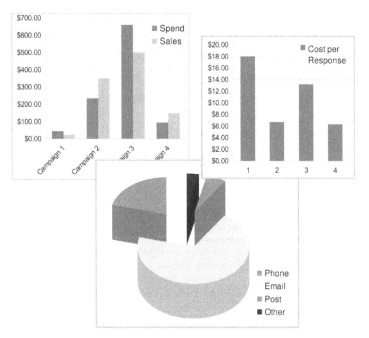

Over time, this information becomes more and more valuable as the data contributing to it grows and its statistical relevance increases. This data allows the marketers to make a case for their value and their continued budgetary support, and to make continual improvements to the way they spend that budget.

Automation

The most automated part of the marketing process is in the distribution of the communications - for example, in creating letters or assigning phone calls for each of the people in the marketing lists attached to the campaign.

Rather than having the marketer manually create a phone call activity for each person on the marketing list and assign it to an inside sales rep, the CRM application may be able to automate this process. The process of recording campaign responses and taking the next steps to advance the sale may also be automated, but these steps may require additional customization.

The Lack: Email and Social Media

You may notice that much of the functionality that I have mentioned is focused on more traditional methods of communication. Let's talk about email and social media. Most CRM applications have the ability to send out email blasts to a group of leads or contacts, but the functionality is limited compared with that of an email marketing application that's specifically designed for the purpose.

Often, integration with a third party tool is used to bridge the gap between the CRM application and the email marketing tool. Functionality included in an email marketing tool that's absent from a CRM application may include cross browser testing, spam score testing, email template building, and more.

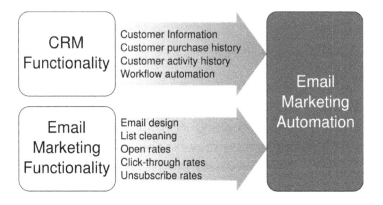

These third party tools also provide metrics that track open and click through rates for the emails you send, and duration and details about the prospect's visits to your website. These metrics can then be used to build automated lead routing or lead scoring rules that help you prioritize the people with whom you choose to proactively follow up, as well as helping you determine the most appropriate method of follow up.

For example, let's say that your marketing team sends out an email to 250 leads from CRM. 50 of them opened the email you sent. Ten of them clicked on a link. Three of those actually downloaded the white paper you were offering. Understanding that it costs your company very little to continue emailing these leads, and that it costs much more to have a salesperson begin personally following up with them, which of these leads would you throw over the wall to sales?

These process are called "Lead Scoring" and "Lead Routing." With email marketing applications that integrate with CRM, you can have this type of insight. To some degree, it's not until you have these features that you're truly engaged in "marketing automation."

But for many, email marketing is now an antiquated concept. Unfortunately, the market leading CRM applications are currently without strong functionality built around what many consider the primary communication method of the future: social media. Again, third party tools may help bridge the gap, but the current state of the market is such that this functionality is still in its definition stage.

There aren't many third party tools that deliver social media marketing integration with CRM, and those that do provide some functionality don't necessarily originate from a strong understanding of how social media marketing strategy will integrate into the existing CRM strategy.

The jury is still out on how social media and CRM applications will operate together in the future, although, if you're an enterprise sized B2C company, you seem to be closer than others to getting a definition clear enough to justify taking action. The next few years will be exciting for those hoping for greater development and clarity to come to this strategy.

CRM for Service (Service Automation)

Out of the box, customer service in CRM centers around the ability to keep track of cases and the way in which your company responded. At your company, you may refer to cases as incidents, or tickets, or service requests.

This is the area of CRM that we in Europe and North America have, almost universally, had direct exposure to. We've all called a company with a complaint or a problem related to their product or service. Sometimes the experience was a positive one, with a quick and effective resolution. Other times... Don't even get me started.

The worst is when you call in, and the person you speak to asks for your name, your account number, and some other information to verify your identity, and *then* asks you why you're calling, and then tells you he or she can't handle that and transfers you to another person, who asks you for your name, your account number, and some other information to verify your identity. If that second person, now that you're at the 20 minute mark with hold times, tells you that your problem isn't their department, your head's just going to explode. And sometimes, after your head explodes, you realize that they just transferred you back to the first person you spoke to.

The difference between the positive and the nightmarish scenario is, in large measure, the effective use of CRM. The CRM application's service automation capabilities generally center around the following areas:

Account/Customer Information

The first thing a customer service rep needs to know is who's calling. In the nightmare I described above, they even asked for my identifying information before they made sure that I had reached the right service center. The customer information in the hands of the service reps is one of the things that make it possible for a customer to feel like his/her experience with the company is a consistent one. I remember the day when you would call a company's service line and you would have to tell them which products you owned, give them a serial number , which still happens, and a bunch of other stuff that they wouldn't have any excuse to not know in the year 2011. When a customer calls a service line, he should speak to someone who has a full understanding of his history of interactions with the company, including his purchases and past requests for service.

I'm speaking about customer service over the phone because of its universal relevance, but the customer service call center is actually a declining institution. There are still plenty of them around, and any large company has one, but companies are increasingly offering support via other channels, including email, chat, and now, social media. But in any of these channels, the ability to identify a customer and understand that customer's history of interactions with the company is crucial to effective customer service.

The word "case" is funny. It always makes me think of the kind of case that a private investigator like Magnum PI would solve. Maybe that's what you have to do when you're working in a service center, pretend like you're a PI trying to get to the bottom of something. I had a job at a call center once while I was waiting to go to college. I lasted about three weeks. Anyway, I wasn't working any cases, but if I had been, the excitement may have enabled me to stick it out a little longer.

If your company doesn't call them cases, they're probably called tickets or service requests. If you don't call them cases, maybe you should think about it. The idea is to keep track of the customer's initiation of this thing, and to then track it to its conclusion.

The case may have a type, for example, it could be a complaint, a request for information, or a request for a replacement part. This is tracked on the case. The case has a time when it was opened, and it has a time when it's closed, or resolved. The elapsed time is probably tracked proactively in order to make sure that your customer service response times are in the range you've targeted. The case may also allow you to record the level of satisfaction the customer expresses at the end when the case is closed, which would allow you to rate your overall satisfaction level, or that of a particular team, individual, or even get an aggregate satisfaction level of cases related to a particular product.

Contract Tracking

A case may be something that a customer has to pay for, unless the customer is under contract. If the customer is under contract, they may have a certain number of cases they can open on that contract, for example, they may be allowed four cases per year. The CRM application should be able to automate the process of keeping track of those four allotted cases and disallowing them from opening up a fifth. It should similarly be able to keep track of allotted minutes, if the service time is measured that way instead of with a count of cases. A case may take a certain number of minutes, and that time can be decremented from the allotment to which the customer is contractually entitled.

Some service offerings involve more than flipping a switch in a database, answering a question via phone, or authorizing a shipment of a replacement part. For example, my brother in law works for a company that sells industrial blowers. They go inside of a pipe and blow air through the pipe. In this industry, when a customer has a problem, there are two ways of servicing that customer: first, to go on site, or second, to have the customer ship the blower back to the reseller so the reseller can fix it at their service location. In either instance, there are a few conceivable complexities when scheduling the service.

1. First of all, there are a limited number of technicians who can service the blower. These technicians need to be available; not scheduled for another request, not on vacation, not at a training, and not doing anything else.

2. Second, there are certain tools that need to be available. There may be only one of the tools that's required for a certain type of service, although there are more than one service technicians. If the service being scheduled requires that tool, then there are

two contingencies that need to be considered; the technician and the tool.

3. In more complicated scenarios, there may be multiple skill sets between technicians and multiple tools. For instance, a certain service may require three of the seven skills that are available among the technicians, and two particular tools. To schedule this service, one would need to find a time where one technician or a combination of technicians who had the three required skills would be available at the same time the two tools were available.

This type of logic can easily get beyond even the smartest person, especially when there are a reasonably large number of service requests coming in. The human brain isn't designed to quickly process this type of computation, but CRM software is. Or, at least some CRM applications are.

Automation

Much of the automation involved in the customer service process, other than the service scheduling intelligence I just described, occurs in the routing of and reminders about cases. When a case is received, it may be placed in a queue for someone to pick up, or it may be automatically assigned based on its characteristics. When the case has been open for a certain amount of time without resolution or update, it may be reassigned or it may generate a reminder to the assigned service representative. These types of automation can help a service department meet their desired service response times and satisfaction levels.

Conclusion

As I mentioned at the beginning, the three pillars discussed here, Sales, Marketing, and Service, are not the only three areas of the business where CRM can add value. Beyond integrating with back office systems, a CRM solution can also address unique business needs that don't naturally fit into a back office system, but aren't part of the three pillars of CRM either.

Companies often engage in custom development to build line of business applications to address these needs. The "Advanced Vendor Considerations" chapter has a section that discusses using CRM as a platform for this type of development, as well as discussing the smaller scale customizations that can make the CRM application a more effective tool for the execution of your business strategy.

Finding a Solution

CRM is Not a Car.
Don't Buy it Like it's a Car.

Despite those television commercials about incredibly intelligent and capable people being intimidated by the thought of buying a car, I use this example in the title because I think everyone knows the process of buying a car, and some of the key things to consider. Buying a car is a matter of defining a number of preferences, including make, model, color and options. You weigh what you want with what it costs.

Unlike CRM, a car is not a solution, it's a product. I mean, if you want to play semantics you could say it's a solution to the problem of having to walk everywhere. You're losing money on shoes and you want to plug that budget leak by buying a car, and the money you spend on depression medication because you can't get a date... no, I can't even stretch to make a good argument. Buying a car is buying a product, and the decision to buy a product is starkly different than the decision to buy a solution.

Unfortunately, you and many others have been exposed to forums where nobody understands that. And if you weren't careful, you may have bought in to the false premises underlying the whole conversation. For example, if you're a member of any LinkedIn groups relating to sales, or technology, or probably many other categories, you may have seen discussions that look something like this:

Mark: My company is looking for CRM. What are your recommendations/ experiences/ good/ bad/ concerns?

Jake: You only need to look at one system - SALESFORCE.COM!!!!!

Rob: Some free ones include Zoho and Sugar. I think Vtiger is another free one.

Sandy: I hate CRM.

Nathan: Do your users use Outlook? Microsoft Dynamics CRM has the best Outlook integration on the market.

Denise: Please feel free to check out my company's solution. It's a low monthly cost and it gives you the best solution, anywhere on the planet, hands down. We don't have a website yet, but if you want to talk send me an email at dj@gmail.com.

***** 15 other similar comments *****

Mark: Thank you all for your excellent comments. I'm starting the formal process of evaluating and I'm excited to share what I find.

Jake: SALESFORCE.COM!!!!!

Manny: Salesforce is totally cheap and awesome.

Derek: Salesforce? Cheap?? What Salesforce are you talking about?

Tom: Sugar works for me. I have 8 companies where I'm the only employee and

I never have any problems. It helps if you know SQL and PHP. I can write batch files that update the database with different values depending on list imports using system time and AJAX.

Mark: Thanks again for all of your feedback. I'm overwhelmed, really! I've looked at all of those that I could, and we've gone ahead with CRMZ. It was the best for us because it has a spot for YouTube.

Jake: What!? No SALESFORCE.COM?????

Lars: ACT! is what we use. We have a small user base and it's not online so we can't get to the data out of the office but it stores contacts centrally which is good.

Lance: My company has a software that lets you build your own CRM system based on your own requirements, so it's totally custom to your needs. Let me know if you want to talk.

Randy: I suggest we get together to talk. Are you free this afternoon or tomorrow morning? I can walk you through your choices and let me tell you there are some bad ones. I've seen people wish for death instead of a long life with the CRM system they chose. Whatever you do, don't go with CRMZ. Here's my number: 555-964-0034.

Randy: Oh, sorry, just saw your post from 3 months ago. I wish you success! CRMZ is a great product. Give me a call if you need help, I've done more implementations than I can count 555-964-0034.

And on and on. This conversation takes place in other venues as well, but I use the LinkedIn example because it's a venue that you're probably familiar with. If you go to the Answers area on LinkedIn and search for "CRM", you'll see a huge list of discussions like the one above. The largest tops out at 101 answers!

This is great information if you're doing consumer research, but remember, CRM is a solution, not simply a product. It's a strategy with supporting tools, designed to solve a problem. The CRM software application is simply one of those supporting tools, and it's worthless without the strategy backing it, just like a hammer is useless if you don't want to pound any nails. Because it's a solution, the question of which vendor's application you should use isn't even relevant until you've defined your strategy and the functionality required to support it.

Once you know those things, you're light years beyond those guys in the LinkedIn groups.

You Don't Know What You Don't Know

Now let's make a pragmatic distinction: when I say that the process of defining requirements comes before the vendor decision, I'm over simplifying things a little bit. In a real world CRM implementation today, you will most likely develop your requirements with the help of vendors or their consulting partners, unless you have no budget and you're determined to do this internally. In which case, I hate to tell you, but... just look two to three years down the road for the time when you'll be doing this again, and apply this advice there. And make sure you have a budget that time.

As I stated in the Introduction, *there's a good possibility that more than one CRM vendor's application could deliver your solution perfectly well*.

CRM software technology has become commoditized to the point that the applications from many vendors share a common set of core functionality.

The problem with the position you stand in as someone searching for a solution is that *you don't know what that functionality is*. You may know a part of it, and if you're the guy with no budget, you may even be tempted to say you could try to go learn it, but as people who hire consultants often say, you don't know what you don't know. And those things that you don't know are unquestionably very important to your solution. The job of the consulting partner or someone in a similar capacity from a vendor is to help uncover your requirements and to architect a solution that will meet them. If the partner is good, they will zoom out another step and insist on understanding how the requirements tie back to the strategy that they came from, and may even suggest additional requirements that you hadn't thought of yourself.

During this process, you may come to a point where you realize that the solution being proposed by a vendor or their partner can't fulfill your requirements. So you begin searching for another one who can, or, if you're being courted by multiple vendors/partners, you just cross that one off the list and continue with the others. In this way, you define the requirements during the process of selecting a vendor.

Can you see the error in focusing solely on the vendor like Mark did in the LinkedIn group example above? He never found out what he didn't know. He probably still doesn't know today. When you engage the expertise necessary to develop and evaluate your strategy and requirements, you stand a much better chance of purchasing a solution that will help you succeed. There's a chance you'll look over at another solution that you didn't choose afterward, jump to the edge of your chair, and say "Shoot! It would have been cool to have that GPS module on the account that gives our reps voice directions to our customers."

But if you're wise, you'll realize that the reason you didn't think of that during your decision making process is because it wasn't part of your core strategy or requirements. And so you'll sit back again, contented that you have a solution that's adding real value to your company, even if it doesn't have every bell and whistle that exists on the market.

A Qualification

I'm going to nuance this discussion once again by making another pragmatic distinction: I said that because CRM software had become commoditized, many vendors share a common set of core functionality. That's true of those vendors who can be seen as leaders in the market. In reality, CRM has become *so* commoditized that one couldn't possibly catalog all of the CRM software offerings available, simply because they probably can't all be found by one person.

There are literally hundreds of CRM applications on the market. So when I say there are multiple vendors whose applications could meet your needs, read me carefully and don't assume that I mean *any* vendor can meet your needs. As a matter of fact, if you have a reasonably high set of expectations, most of them can't. So vendor choice does matter!

In the next chapter, we'll begin talking about some of the things that distinguish vendors and their CRM offerings from each other.

Choosing a Vendor: Flawed Decision Criteria

So far, we've established that many people buy CRM software with an inappropriate focus on the vendor.

This focus is inappropriate because it causes people to overlook the more important aspects of a project, like finding outside expertise to help flesh out a strategy and the CRM solution requirements that will properly support that strategy.

When people have this myopic approach to purchasing CRM, they assume that the vendor whose application has the most features, the best price, or the most votes in an online survey must be the one that will meet their needs. This is a mistake.

That's not to say that the piece of software in question couldn't be part of an appropriate solution, the problem is that they just don't know.

A solution is something that's defined beforehand, something with parameters, something that specifically addresses recognized, documented, and properly understood problems. People who just get the CRM itch, thinking they need it but not knowing why, are not properly prepared.

Of course, the vendor decision does need to be made. In this chapter, we'll talk about some common decision criteria that *really shouldn't be used the way they are*.

I'm not saying that the things on this list aren't appropriate considerations, because they certainly can be. But they're usually used in ways that negatively impact the chances for success. In the next chapter, we'll talk about some important decision criteria that you should make sure to consider.

Price

Of course price is important. If you can't afford it, you can't afford it. If you're a 50 person company with a budget of $30,000 and someone's trying to sell you SAP, you're probably going to run into issues. However, price is often misused as a decision criteria. If you read the last chapter, you read the mock LinkedIn discussion started by Mark.

Mark asked for CRM recommendations from the members of the group, and a good chunk of those recommendations came back with price as their main topic. "Zoho is free." "Sugar is free."

When free options are present in the mix, it often causes the person doing the investigation to narrow his/her search prematurely, or to slide the expectations of what he will pay or is willing to pay, or what he considers a reasonable price, downward.

The problem with this is that he may rule out the vendors whose applications would allow him to develop the best possible solution. Worse still, he may begin to expect that his *solution* will be free or very low cost. Not just the CRM software *product*, but the *solution*. And of course, at this point, his connection with reality is quickly on the wane.

Many of the free software applications have no partners or a limited number of partners who offer implementation consulting. It's understandable, after all, people who want free software can't be willing to spend very much money on an implementation project, can they? But in actuality, most of this software isn't truly "free" anyway. It's free in some limited way, but the vendor still has to make money.

Something like Zoho CRM, for example, is free for a few users, but if you need more than that, you're paying. Sugar CRM is open source, so it's free if you want to take the software and put it on your own servers, but it costs money if you want to subscribe to an on demand service.

Even Salesforce.com has a cheap option; it just doesn't do very much. At the time of writing, their prices range from $5 to $250[a] per user, per month; quite a spread. Try to guess their strategy in that pricing model. It's the same as most of these "free" vendors.

Everybody's familiar with the phrase "You get what you pay for." And every last one of us hopes, on a

---

a   www.salesforce.com/crm/editions-pricing.jsp
    Accessed January 26, 2011.

regular basis, that it's not true in our particular circumstance. But if I break this to you now, maybe it won't hurt as much as if you'd held on to that hope a bit longer. It's true when buying CRM. You get what you pay for. I'm not saying you can't obtain a good solution using a "free" piece of CRM software, I'm just saying that it's not going to be free.

But why should it be? If you're properly prepared, unlike Mark on LinkedIn, you're looking for a solution that will help your company sell more, market more effectively, and retain more customers, a solution that will automate manual, repetitive, time consuming sales tasks that have both a real cost and an opportunity cost, a solution that will help your marketing department generate more or better leads and make more effective use of their budget. In short, you're looking for a solution that will help your company make more money. When was the last time you got something like that for free?

Of course, if you're a three man organization just looking for a place to centrally store contacts, accounts, and opportunities, then by all means, go for the gratis, and read no further.

For the rest of you, the best advice I can give regarding price is to be realistic. Look for the solution first. Once you find the right solution, price it. If you can't afford it, at least you know the cost of fixing your problems. You may be able to find another similar solution for a lower price from a different vendor or partner. But even if you can't, you're far better off than you would have been had you somehow become convinced during your CRM search that your problems weren't important enough to make you spend any money.

Popularity

Another big fallacy in evaluating CRM applications is what I'll call the Prom Queen Fallacy. With the benefit of hindsight, how many of you would want to be married today to the person elected king or queen at your high school prom, or even just date them? A lot of you would probably say that you wouldn't want to. But of course, you didn't know that back at your prom. You were one of the guys standing along the wall day dreaming about saving her life, or one of the girls standing next to those guys, thinking about going to the salon the very next day to get your hair done like hers.

Everyone has had an experience like that in one form or another. If it wasn't a prom queen, it could have been a 1986 Ford Mustang or a hairstyle that is no longer documented anywhere on this planet because you destroyed every last shred of evidence of its existence. The point is that at the time, the prevailing winds of popularity kept you from discerning the truth about something.

When you evaluate CRM, the same thing can happen, if you're not careful. The reason is sort of the same, as the popularity of a CRM application has no necessary correlation to its effectiveness in accomplishing the objectives for which it was implemented. There are at least two reasons for this:

1. Popularity is an end user phenomenon

2. Popularity is a marketing phenomenon

Popularity is an end user phenomenon

This may sound counter intuitive. If the people who use the CRM application *really like it,* doesn't that mean it's a good application? The answer is "kind of."

Remember, if you're doing this right, you're not evaluating CRM products, you're evaluating CRM solutions. In that respect, if you really wanted to weigh the experience of the vendors' past customers, you wouldn't talk to the end users. You would talk to the people who had ownership of the CRM initiative, the people who were accountable for solving certain problems or achieving certain objectives, and who chose to do so by implementing a CRM solution. Those are the people who can most identify with you and your situation today.

Imagine that you purchase and deploy CRM, and you have ten, sixty five, or two hundred people at your company using it. During the deployment, you spend time working with a consulting partner to define your objectives and understand how the CRM technology can support your business strategy. You make decisions based on how the software can adapt to your needs. You get to know the product from an executive level.

Now imagine that it's several months or years down the road. You've seen the results of your efforts, good or bad. You remember the decisions you made at the beginning and how they've played out in your ability to execute your strategy, good or bad.

And, if applicable, you remember how certain decisions which weren't ideal had to be made because of software limitations. Or, maybe you remember that the software actually brought capabilities to the table that allowed you to do more than you had originally thought possible. Now, imagine someone else wanting to know whether or not the CRM application you used was a good choice. Who is best equipped to give them an accurate answer? You, or a sales guy who's been at your company for six months?

None of those end users were there in those meetings. Most of them weren't aware of the strategy and requirements driving the CRM implementation. Many of them had no awareness whatsoever that the problems you were trying to solve even existed. They simply are not equipped to comment on the true value of the CRM application and its contribution to your CRM solution. They can only comment on whether or not it was a pleasant experience for them as end users.

Is the end user experience important? Absolutely! A CRM solution without happy end users is a host to all kinds of attendant ills. We'll talk about user adoption later in this chapter. But the fact that a vendor's application makes end users happy doesn't mean that it can carry the day with your business strategy. Maybe it can, but you need to figure that out first. When you assume that a CRM application is right for you simply because it's popular, you're putting the proverbial cart before the horse.

Popularity is a Marketing Phenomenon

This will be short. I shouldn't have to write this in a book on how to choose a good product, but I do. So here it is: the company that has the best marketing doesn't always have the best product. They usually are, however, the most popular.

If what you're looking for when choosing a CRM application is inclusion in a user group, or a sense of community, or the prestige of owning an application from a certain vendor, or the aura of success, or the excuse to go to vendor conferences, or the warm fuzzies you get from reading the vendor's website or banner ads, then at least be honest with yourself and admit it.

You don't have to read any further here. My advice doesn't relate to any of those emotional needs. I can tell you this though; none of that is going to make your business more successful.

That being said, popularity isn't totally irrelevant. A CRM application that's wildly popular probably isn't an absolute piece of junk. You can ascertain that much. I mentioned earlier that it's a good idea to stick with the market leaders. Those products all have a relatively strong card in the popularity deck; they will each play that card to their greatest possible advantage.

Just remember, popularity has no direct correlation on the quality of the solution, because it's an end user phenomenon, and because it's the result of marketing.

Conclusion

In this chapter, I've argued that price and popularity are certain factors that have their proper place in your evaluation of a CRM application. They often, however, play an inappropriate role in evaluations, and are given undue emphasis. In the next chapter, we'll discuss some more relevant decision criteria that should come into play before price and popularity are seriously considered.

Choosing a Vendor: Appropriate Decision Criteria

There are certainly vendor considerations that may be very relevant in your search for the best CRM solution. These should be explored and discussed throughout the investigation process, as they may have a strong role in your strategy and the necessary solution.

In this chapter, we'll discuss the following considerations:

1. Deployment Type

2. Methods of Access

3. User Friendliness

4. Company Strength and Product Roadmap

5. Your Partner

Deployment Type: On-Premise and Cloud

The rapid change that has taken place in the technology landscape during the last several years has made this an important topic. There are two main deployment categories; on-premise and in the cloud. Some people have predicted that it's just a matter of time before the cloud becomes the only method of software delivery. Whether that's true or not, it's far enough out that you should carefully consider your choice; either one has the possibility of delivering strong value for years to come if it's the right choice for you right now.

In addition, vendors that offer both methods of deployment will most likely allow you to transition from one to another if future necessity dictates that you do so.

What is the difference between On-Premise and the Cloud?

During the past several decades, the traditional delivery model for software in the business has been on-premise. A company usually has a stack of servers somewhere in the office where the business applications run, and the people in the office can get to those applications through the company's intranet. These people's computers had to be on their company's internal network to get to these applications.

The next wave of technology allowed the company's employees to reach their applications when they were outside of the office, and therefore not on the company's network. Since, at this point, the applications didn't need to be hosted on a server inside the company's office building anymore, the next logical step was for the applications to be hosted somewhere else.

Technologies such as multi-tenancy and server virtualization allowed vendors or hosting companies to host applications very economically. The resulting business model has been to offer software via a subscription, or in other words, to offer *software as a service*. You may have seen the acronym SaaS, which people often pronounce "sass", which is a term that, in popular usage, is synonymous with "the cloud."

If you take a step back and think about it, the cloud really wasn't as new to you as you thought it was when you first heard the term. If you've ever used an email service like Hotmail or Yahoo, you were using a cloud email service. The revolutionary concept that's been making waves in the last several years has been the possibility of hosting business class software in the cloud.

Cloud vs. On-Premise: Price as the Decision Criteria

The decision between on-premise and cloud deployment really comes down to a few factors. The first is price. The cloud is inseparable from the economics of software delivery. As a matter of fact, the level of interest in the cloud and the pace of its adoption over the last several years have received a tremendous boost from the global recession we've been experiencing. On-premise software is *licensed* to a company and its users. You've probably read that in an end user license agreement before, where it says "this software is licensed, not sold."

The company pays a considerable fee for the necessary licenses to use the software. The licenses are usually related to the number of users that will have access to the software or the number of servers the software will be installed on, or some other similar criteria.

Since the software is a considerable investment, it's unacceptable for the purchasing company to buy this year's version of the software, and then have to buy the next version all over again when it comes out two years later. To address this injustice, most software companies have long since created a plan that allows customers to pay a maintenance fee every year that entitles them to any new versions that come out after their original purchase.

When vendors started offering software in the cloud, many of them introduced startling price differences into the marketplace. Software that had an on-premise license fee of $10,000 may now be offered for $50 a month in the cloud. The level of commitment required to start using a piece of software seemed to be greatly reduced. And in an economy where things changed so fast, and companies that seemed to be pillars of stability shut their doors, less commitment was really attractive.

Can you believe Mervyn's[a] doesn't exist anymore? That may be good for my social life, but think of the horrible cost to my sense of permanence. For those of us who only shop at one store, those kinds of events can cause a level of upheaval you multi-store shoppers simply don't understand.

However, there are some caveats to the "cloud software costs less" principle. The equation usually goes something like this:

Cloud is better because the cloud service costs less than software license fees, software maintenance fees, servers, IT maintenance and other setup and running costs.

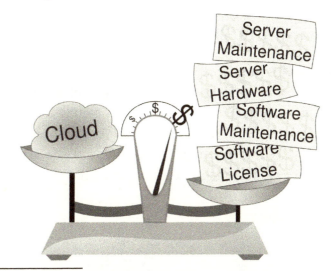

a   Mervyn's was a low end department store in the USA. It went out of business in 2008, along with Circuit City and some of the other major chains that succumbed to the recession following the housing and financial market crash of 2007-08.

Yes, it's obvious that the initial cash outlay is much less for cloud software. However, in many situations, it's currently still cheaper in the long run to have on-premise software. With cloud software, you pay a smaller monthly fee, but you pay it for the rest of your *life*, if you happen to like it that much.

Of course, on-premise software has ongoing costs as well. But if you factor in things like the depreciation of hardware, the cost of network maintenance, and all of the tangential cost factors of on-premise software that we're not going to go into here, you could possibly still come out ahead with on-premise software in the TCO (Total Cost of Ownership) calculation. It depends on what software you're talking about.

Those with greater economical wherewithal than I possess may predict a continuing decline in the cost of software delivered in the cloud, and the time may come when the TCO calculation tips universally and permanently in favor of the cloud. Whether we've reached that point or not is hard to say.

Cloud vs. On-Premise: Maintenance as the Decision Criteria

The second factor in the on-premise vs. cloud decision is maintenance. You're going to see some overlap in this factor with price, naturally, because maintenance costs money. When we're considering this factor, we include the maintenance on the server and the maintenance on all of the software that makes the server run.

In the context of our discussion about CRM software, you're looking at the CRM application itself, an operating system, a database application, and a web server application at the very least. All of these applications require patches and upgrades from time to time. Sometimes something might break and cost you time. This maintenance has to be performed on an ongoing basis.

Many companies see great value in being able to take this maintenance responsibility away from their IT employees and free them up for more useful work.

Cloud vs. On-Premise: Access as the Decision Criteria

The third factor is really less of a factor than it was at one time. When you access an application in the cloud, it's logical to think "I can get to this application anywhere I have an internet connection!" That's true, but it's also probably true of that application's on-premise counterpart, if one exists.

The main reason for on-premise applications not being available outside of the office network is usually an IT policy rather than an inability in the application. However, the methods of granting users outside of the network access to internal applications are becoming more and more secure, and as long as a company's policy allows external users access to an application, the end user will not know the difference.

Cloud vs. On-Premise: Understanding Multi-Tenancy

Back when you started using Hotmail or AOL, you may have said to yourself "this is great, but I'm not sure I'm comfortable with the multi-tenant architecture upon which this application is built." Well, you didn't think they were going to give your inbox its own server, did you!?

A multi-tenant architecture simply means that different users of the program, or, in business class software, different organizations which may each have multiple users, all share some things behind the scenes on the hardware. The separation between users or organizations is not physical, it's logical, meaning that the emails in the inbox of your SaaS email account are possibly stored in a database, in rows that *actually touch other peoples' emails*! Or it means that the services running the application are shared with other users or organizations.

The term "logical separation" means that the email application knows how to retrieve your emails from the database and show them to you, even though they're not physically separated from other peoples' mail. Some people may worry about this being less secure than an architecture where all of a single customer's data were in one place with its own little wall built around it, and it may be. But there are many variables that impact the security of data, and a secure multi-tenant application can be very safe.

There's really not a lot more to know about it from your perspective. In the cloud, you'll be sharing resources behind the scenes. It's the vendor's job to make sure those resources serve everyone efficiently, as you will see in the discussion on Service Level Agreements a few pages ahead. That's why some things, like bandwidth and storage, come at a premium from some vendors.

Methods of Access

This consideration is increasingly important as companies expect greater flexibility to work on the go or in non traditional locations. The two main methods of access other than the standard method of using your PC or laptop while it's connected to the internet are:

Offline Access

Some vendors allow users to "go offline" with their data, or, in other words, to work in the CRM application when they are not connected to the internet and therefore, not connected to the CRM application. These users can create, read, update, and delete data just as they would when connected to the application via the internet, but the data is actually stored locally on the user's laptop. When the user has access again to the internet, he or she can synchronize with the CRM application and the changes made when offline will be pushed into the CRM database.

This method of access is valuable when a company's users are frequently without internet access, such as field service representatives on site at a customer location with no internet, or sales reps who spend a lot of time on planes and would like to use the down time to update CRM.

Mobile Access

Some vendors have a mobile version of their CRM application as well, or have allowed third parties to develop a mobile version. This method of access has become more and more popular as our personal computing habits have become increasingly mobile. It's predicted that the mobile device will become the primary computing device for most people in the coming years. This being the case, it makes sense that an application like CRM, which is commonly used by mobile employees such as salespeople and field service reps, be available on a mobile device.

If you're looking for mobile access, make sure you understand the cost of the extra service. Some vendors charge extra for mobile access, others offer it for free.

User Friendliness

You've probably heard someone site the statistic that some huge percentage of CRM implementations fail due to poor user adoption. I've been hearing that statistic for years, so I know it's old, and I doubt it's being updated on a regular basis. However, the principle is true; a CRM application is worthless when the people who are supposed to use it... don't. Or, they have to use it but they hate it, a scenario that's perhaps a level of magnitude worse than simple inactivity. *That* could lead to the creation of a workplace morale reminiscent of the early scenes of the old movie Joe vs. the Volcano.

The good news is that the world of CRM vendors is well aware of the problem with user adoption, and has been for years. The offerings of many vendors have become easier to use and understand. This necessary change has come not simply from the ever growing ability to design a more attractive user interface, but more importantly, from a shift in the way software is designed. In the early days of CRM, software was primarily created to make a business more profitable and it attempted to achieve this objective from the top down. The objectives focused on the group rather than the individual, which meant that if having information in a database would make the company more successful, then having a room of drones entering that information into the system was a necessary step to achieving that success. The feelings of that group of drones were not a prioritized consideration. Software was focused on delivering benefits to management and those making important decisions, as well as on attempting to standardize customer interactions by creating standard processes encoded in the software. The focus on the end user had yet to mature.

However, the world of software has changed dramatically in the last several decades. To be successful, any software, business focused or otherwise, is expected to deliver greater productivity to the user, packaged in a nice looking, ear tingling, pleasant smelling user experience.

The commoditization of PCs for sale to home users created a market for home software applications, which, because of the relative technical ineptitude of most home users, had to be easy to use and very intuitive. We've all experienced the advances that have been made on that front. If you're like me, some of your first memories of computers were playing Oregon Trail on the Apple IIe, or typing a word processing document on a black screen with green letters. Remember Doogie Howser typing in his journal at the end of every episode?.

Business software, as you might expect, has been required, sometimes (often) against its will, to keep pace with home software in the march toward a positive user experience. After all, how can anyone reasonably expect someone to come to work and use software that's significantly more difficult than what they use at home, simply because the vendor didn't think the end user was important?

Other factors have also pushed software in the direction of greater usability. The younger generations in the workplace are much more mobile than the older ones. Remember that statistic you heard in college about the average number of times people your age would change careers? It seems like that number continues to rise with each new generation that enters the workplace. The time and money required for training on software applications that are difficult to use and take a long time to learn makes it less feasible for a company to employ such programs.

This is particularly true for CRM software, because of the type of business professionals that typically use the system. Many CRM users will not be drones following an on screen phone script or performing some limited number of brainless tasks; the type of employee that would be easy to train when turnover occurred. Rather, they are highly skilled employees, such as sales, marketing, and field service professionals, who need an application that supports their independent work habits.

It's imperative that the CRM application be easy to use and intuitive to reduce the training required for new employees and to contribute to the happiness of the employees who use it.

Notice that I didn't say "eliminate the need for training." MOST companies make the egregious mistake of skimping on CRM training for their end users. Ample, high quality training is one of the easiest steps a company can take to promote user adoption. This doesn't mean scheduling four solid days of training. A useful article at CIO.com[14] outlines a great set of training best practices. If your partner doesn't operate according to these principles, you can request that they do so with your company

In addition, as these younger generations have entered the workplace, the environment has become increasingly democratized. While this would never have happened several decades ago, today there are frequent situations where one or more employees refuse to use software that a boss has directed them to use. This sometimes even leads the boss to scrap the software rather than start a prolonged scrap with his employees over whether or not they must use the application he's mandated.

So when I say user friendliness, I'm talking about this shift in the way software is developed, and for what reason. The current leaders in the CRM industry understand the need to add value to the end user and to the organization as a whole.

A CRM application must be able to make an organization more intelligent, more serviceable to customers, and more nimble. These are the organizational benefits. And, it must make the end users more productive. If it's being used by a salesperson, it must help that salesperson sell more so he or she can earn more money. If it's being used by a marketing or customer service professional, that person must be able to achieve improved individual performance. The truth is that no software application that's intended to be widely used within an organization can succeed without doing this.

How Friendly Is the Application?

Some things you may want to keep in mind when evaluating an application on the user friendliness scale:

Integration with Applications Already in Use

Which software applications do your end users already use? Can the CRM applications that you're using interface with these applications to deliver a more streamlined user experience? The obvious application to consider in here is Microsoft Office Outlook. Most CRM vendors offer some level of integration with Outlook, although the quality varies from vendor to vendor.

The intention of connecting CRM and Outlook can be generally defined as follows: people use CRM to track information about customers, including interactions that have happened or are scheduled to happen, such as a phone call, a meeting, a task to provide some required paperwork, etc. People use Outlook to schedule, communicate, and create reminders. By connecting the two programs, the end user gains the ability to push scheduling and communication items such as emails, appointments and tasks up to CRM so they are visible to others and tracked in a central, organized location. They also gain the ability to receive Outlook tasks and appointments and reminders that are created automatically in CRM by a work flow or other type of automation.

While Outlook is the most obvious nominee, there are others that can also add significant value when integrated with CRM.

Does your company use unified communications or an external phone system that could be integrated with CRM? Does your marketing department work in an email marketing tool or social media marketing tool that could benefit from receiving CRM data and that could provide valuable data back to CRM?

While many of these types of integrations would require third party functionality or a specific customization to integrate with CRM, they should certainly be a part of your evaluation. Be aware of all of the possible ways CRM could add value to your organization, and don't be overly dismissive.

The integration I'm discussing here in this section is limited to applications that are end user focused. We'll talk later about the potential of integrating CRM into your company's existing technology stack, including the enterprise applications like ERP.

Application Speed

This is, of course, one of the first things you'll notice in a demo. You don't want your users sitting around waiting for screen loads while they could be out selling or doing other work. Make sure you understand what you can reasonable expect from the application.

If you're investigating an on-premise application, it's likely that most of the speed considerations will depend on your hardware and your internal network, although a higher quality application will be able to make better use of hardware to provide a fast interface with less demanding hardware requirements. If you're looking at a cloud application, the majority of the responsibility to create a speedy application rests with the vendor, although the quality of your internet connection is also very important.

Cloud Only SLAs (Service Level Agreements)

Cloud software providers, especially those selling into the upper SMB and Enterprise business markets, are increasingly providing specific service level agreements to their customers. The SLA is usually expressed in terms of an "up time" or "availability" percentage such as 99.9%. You'll often hear this figure expressed in "nines", with the question being how many nines a cloud software provider can guarantee. The preceding percentage can be referred to as "three nines." This percentage represents the amount of time that the application is guaranteed to be "up", meaning available and properly functioning. Even a 99.9% up time means about 8 hours of downtime per year.

No vendor can truly guarantee that their application will be available *all of the time*, and they really can't guarantee that their application will be available a certain percentage of the time either. The point of an SLA is to gauge the vendor's commitment to the customer.

That being the case, you're only interested in SLAs to which a vendor has made a financial commitment, meaning that the vendor will discount or refund your service fees when they fail to meet their commitment. This is the only SLA that actually communicates something real about what you can expect from a vendor's application availability.

How Familiar is the Application?

User interface design is an important part of the user friendliness factor of a CRM application. This includes questions like the following:

"How many clicks does it take to get a task done?"

"How is the navigation similar to other applications I use?"

"What color is it?"

And so on...

What color is it?! Yes! It's a small consideration, to be honest, but you have probably been impacted, positively or negatively, by some aesthetic detail of an application you had to spend time in on a regular basis.

My first experience with CRM was when I was working as a salesperson for a small software company, meticulously keeping a record of my activities in an Excel spreadsheet. One day, my boss told me that I would have to give up my spreadsheet and start using something called Salesforce.com. I wasn't so experienced that I revolted at the change from some long entrenched habits, but I did notice several things that I didn't like about my work process in the new application.

One was that I couldn't intuitively understand how to get to the list view, even after several weeks of using the application. Sure, I could get there, but it didn't seem to make sense. I did most of my work with "Leads", and when I clicked on the tab with that name, I didn't see the leads list, I saw something else, some summary type screen that was different than what I expected to see.

Also, unlike my Excel sheet, I couldn't perform in line editing on the items I was working with in the list view, I had to click on the item's row and see the record in a form. Then, I had to click yet again to actually edit the data. Perhaps worst of all, one of the areas in the application where I spent most of my day was a really unlovely puke yellow. I'm probably exaggerating when I say that the yellow was "worst of all", but I didn't like it one bit; I couldn't figure out why anyone would choose a color like that for an application that was designed to be used by a human.

These are the types of reactions you want to avoid from your employees. If they can immediately get that comfortable, at home type of feeling in the CRM application you give them, you have a much better chance of achieving positive user adoption. Unfortunately, that special application is not going to be the same application for everyone. However, it's important that you understand your employees, what applications they are accustomed to working with, and make the familiarity factor a part of your criteria in your search for a CRM program.

Company Strength and Product Roadmap

When choosing the application that will form a key part of your CRM solution and strategy, keep in mind the ever shifting sands of the software corporate landscape. Vendors come and go. The danger is that you build a CRM solution with an application that, for various possible reasons, doesn't keep pace with the rest of the world of technology. The vendor may face financial troubles, get acquired, have poor management decisions... it's hard to say what can happen with a software corporation in today's economy.

I'm acquainted with one company owned by a man named Rick (name changed) that purchased licenses to use a CRM application developed by a large and well established software corporation. After Rick and his company had implemented this CRM application, the corporation they licensed it from sold the CRM program code to another company. Somehow, probably due to a combination of negligence on the part of Rick and poor management by the firm that purchased the CRM program code, Rick's company missed the upgrade window for his version of the application. Today, Rick's company is stuck with a very old

CRM application that can't be upgraded due to incompatibility between the version he purchased originally and the version available now from the company that currently owns the program code.

This particular CRM application was a strong player in the early days of CRM software, and now holds a low to middling position at best. The program code has been owned by at least three different corporations or more, depending on how you see the concept of ownership and the fuzzy lines between companies and people. Any way you look at it, however, it's had a foster child history, and the quality of its offering has been directly impacted.

Siebel CRM is another classic example. At one point the company was riding a wave of success and popularity which broke rather abruptly, helped a bit by the preceding .com bust. After months of pep talks to investors and consumers full of "we're on the way back up" types of statements, Siebel was sold to Oracle.

As you may know, a Siebel CRM implementation is notorious for taking a *really* long time. You typically wouldn't have even looked into that application unless you were a large enterprise and could fund a years long implementation project.

Can you imagine being halfway through such a project and seeing the wheels fall off the company that owned the code for the program you're implementing? Maybe your title at work was "Siebel CRM Administrator." All of a sudden, there's no more Siebel! You've been working on the implementation for a year, and not a single end user has yet used the application. Your levels of on the job stress just went through the roof in one day.

So the point here is this. The health of the CRM vendor's business is important to you. What's their history? What's their stability? What is their commitment to the CRM product? Is it documented, and how far into the future does the documentation reach?

Companies will often produce what's called a "product roadmap" to detail the vision and strategy they intend to follow in future development. Use this document to evaluate the questions in this paragraph, and make a choice that won't make you old before your time.

Your Partner

I've mentioned this previously, but it's an important consideration. The success of your CRM solution will depend upon two main factors; the strategy and the application. Your implementation partner (read: the consulting company that you hire to help you with CRM) has a significant influence on both.

It is therefore critical that you choose a partner who can understand your business, add value to discussions about your strategy and successfully implement the application. A good partner blends business and technical acumen to develop a CRM solution that will give you the results you're hoping for.

Business Acumen

It's great if you can find a partner that has worked with other companies in your industry and of a size similar to yours. That's not always possible, however, and different industries share many common characteristics.

For example, in recent months I've worked with people from companies that perform IT services, sell third party software, and perform green building consulting, who all have a similar need to forecast a residual revenue stream from services delivered over a period of time. In one instance, the company's internal sales forecasting didn't have an established procedure. The company sold software licenses, on going IT support, and one time implementation projects. They hadn't thought through the process of forecasting sales that included these different types of revenue.

Questions like this come up throughout the process of preparing for a CRM implementation. It's crucial for a partner who's familiar with situations like yours to be able to offer solutions, question and critique the ways you've been doing it in the past (if you have been doing it in the past), and help you come up with a procedure for the future.

The proper solution to such questions will have two characteristics:

1. It will help you achieve your business objectives

2. It will be supported by the appropriate software functionality

Again, notice here the necessary fusion between business and technical acumen. By understanding the technical aspects of the CRM application, the partner can suggest approaches to meeting business needs that fully leverage the program's capabilities and deliver the most value to your organization.

There are soft areas of focus here that are important, such as understanding the humans who will use the application and the personalities that typically inhabit different areas of a business that is also very important. Beware of partners who focus too much on technical competence and not enough on business competence. After all, you're looking for a consultant, not simply a technician.

Technical Acumen

This is a simple necessity. It doesn't matter whether you're looking at a vendor whose application is hosted in the cloud or installed on a local server. Anyone with enough time could figure out the steps to installing and/or setting up the program, but making it live and breathe inside of your organization requires a resource with a comprehensive understanding of what's possible.

In addition to technical acumen to map your strategies to the best technology, every CRM application has its quirks, its little things that don't work exactly how one might expect, and its little ins and outs that could cost you time, money, or cause your users to give up. It's important that you have technical expertise assisting in your CRM implementation.

Conclusion

This chapter has outlined some of the decision criteria you should pay attention to when choosing a CRM vendor. There are more than what I've covered here, but hopefully this will get you started. However, I want to emphasize one point that I mentioned in an earlier chapter; a CRM implementation partner can help you immensely as you evaluate vendors. Your task isn't to create an Excel sheet in which you'll compare every CRM vendor on planet earth. Rather, your task is to find a vendor that can deliver a solution that will meet your company's needs. Therefore, I would narrow the vendor question down to two general criteria:

1. Application has functionality that can meet your business requirements

2. Vendor has implementation partner that you trust to help you execute your strategy

If you find a vendor that can say yes to both of these questions, you're at a good spot, one at which many companies buying CRM never arrive, simply because they don't ask the right questions.

Advanced Vendor Considerations

Having covered some of the most important factors you should consider when evaluating CRM vendors in the last chapter, we'll now turn our attention to some of the more political, technical, or otherwise erudite considerations. In this chapter, we'll discuss the following:

1. Vendor Economics

2. CRM as a Development Platform

3. Customization and Business Specific Functionality

4. Integration with the Existing Technology Stack

Vendor Economics

There are those among us (I'm one of them) who prefer to know how the companies we buy things from make their money. For example, I just joined a new gym near my home. It's great because it's less than a mile away, it has a ton of equipment and floor space, as much as any other gym I've been inside of, and it's only $10 a month! I like that price, but I'm baffled at how they can stay in business charging so little when other gyms with less equipment charge at least twice that much. The place certainly isn't as cush as some other gyms, but it's still very nice.

I've had a few thoughts of how they actually make enough money to stay in business, but as I've considered each one, none seemed to have the real answer. For example, they used to ask me, every time I came through the door, if I wanted to buy a supplement drink, and I thought maybe that was their secret. But they stopped doing that after about two weeks, and I don't think that was a personalized decision based on me saying no every time. They were hard selling the personal training for a while, and I thought maybe that was where their real interest lay. But their personal training is a shambles, with only a few regulars and a whole cast of others who never seem to last more than a week, from what I can tell as one who's never purchased personal training.

Unable to understand their revenue model, I keep expecting to see a notice on the door that they're going out of business. But my gym is actually their fifth or sixth location in my city, so I think they do have a viable financial model, inscrutable as it may be to an outsider. If I figure it out before this book is released, I'll let you know how they make their money, but right now I'm at a complete loss, and it's driving me crazy.

Do you feel the same way about CRM vendors? Let's talk about the ways CRM vendors make their money. I'm going to break this discussion into two categories; Cloud and On-Premise Vendors. I want to note one thing before we begin: if you came to me today and asked for my opinion on which delivery model makes the most sense, I would tell you the cloud. You may be surprised that I say that now when you read the section below, because it will seem that I'm fairly critical of the cloud vendor model. I only write this way because the cloud is still new to many of you who may be reading this, and I want to lay out as many of the potential gotchas as possible.

Cloud Vendors

It's fairly obvious that the main difference between traditional software companies and cloud vendors is that rather than banking on the ability to make big sales on a consistent basis, they make a little bit of money at a time, forever. The revenue model is very similar to something else you've probably considered, which is the mobile app store.

When Apple's iPhone app store was released, everyone who had an iPhone was blown away at how cheap (or free) everything was. Most applications were free, or at least had some free version, with extended functionality available for $1 to $3 a month. You thought "how can these guys be making money?" Well, the answer is simple; there are millions of iPhone users, all of whom think $1 to $3 a month is hardly worth sniffing at.

But do the economics really change? Let's take a look at the cost of using cloud CRM. Below is the pricing from a few vendors.

	Vendor A[a]	Vendor B	Vendor C
Cost per user per month[15]	$44	$125	$75
Monthly Cost for a 40 user Deployment	$1,760	$5,000	$3,000
Annual Cost for a 40 user Deployment	$21,120	$60,000	$36,000

This table is instructive for several reasons. A few bucks a month doesn't seem like much up front, but it sure adds up over time. It doesn't end up being more economical unless you can actually realize the economic advantages of some of the harder to calculate benefits of cloud computing, such as reduced cost of IT salary and reduced hardware cost.

Cheaper and Less Headache

Consider this statement, representative of the sentiment and messaging of cloud vendors in general, from Salesforce.com CEO Marc Benioff:

"The software industry grew too greedy, too complex and too out of touch with the customer.

---

a   These figures are taken from three major vendors' price lists, but I have obscured the names of the vendors so as not to imply any advantage that one specific vendor has over another.

Outrageously expensive to buy, costly to maintain and difficult to change, traditional client/server software has failed customers for years."[16]

As I mentioned in an earlier chapter, I don't see much improvement from cloud vendors in the "outrageously expensive" department. Compare this table above with the one below in the on-premise section for a hypothetical cost of on-premise CRM software. While the message of cloud CRM applications is "cheaper" and "less headache", it seems to me that it only truly delivers on the latter.

There are certainly benefits of being in the cloud, and this may add more *value* to a cloud offering, but considering cost alone, the difference is simply a choice between paying now and paying later. If you can pay for on-premise software in installments, you're probably looking at a cost that's very similar to what you would pay for a cloud application, with the key difference being that an installment plan would end when you had paid for the product.

However, "less headache" does have some financial benefits, such as greater flexibility and less commitment. If it takes four years for a cloud CRM application to generate the up front cost of an on-premise solution, and a company or department in question isn't sure it's going to survive in its current format for that long, then the cloud is the clear choice. Market turbulence, a dynamic technology landscape, and other factors can discourage a company from making an investment in a software application that won't pay off for several years. The finance department may also prefer the cash flow benefits of the cloud solution to the lower total cost of ownership, especially if the future is sufficiently uncertain to cast doubt on the actual realization of those savings.

Buying a Service is Different than Buying a Product

When you're considering the cloud vendor's financial model, remember also that you're not buying a product, you're buying a service. When you buy a product, you buy something in a package, and you hope nothing's missing. Usually, it's not, but there have been notable instances in my own distant past where an overlooked "batteries not included" notice on a package caused me an agonizing delay in gratification. Perhaps you've felt that agony as well. In other words, with a product, there's only one line item on your invoice, and you get what you paid for; the product.

The pricing of services, however, is arbitrary, subject to change, and things may be "tacked on" that you weren't expecting. Think of the last time you went to get your oil changed, and noticed on your receipt a "disposal fee" of several dollars. That several dollars isn't included in the price the service station has advertised out on their street sign. They changed your oil for $19.99, but they also did something else. That something else is certainly closely related to changing the oil, and many of those getting their oil changed would argue that it should be included in the price of "oil change." However, the service station considers it separate. There are costs related to this part of the service, and they choose to pass those costs on to you.

Many cloud software vendors operate in similar fashion. Two obvious costs for these vendors that you may see coming your way are **storage** and **bandwidth**. A cloud vendor's software is hosted in a place very similar to the server room at your own office. There's nothing magical about it, it's just bigger.

Thousands and thousands of servers hum along, inaudible beneath the overpowering and constant whoosh of the AC units that keep the room at 68 to 72 degrees. Your data is taking up real space on a real server, and that space is limited. They allot you a certain amount of space, and when you exceed that allotment, they pass the cost for the extra space on to you.

Those charges could be reasonable, or they could be exorbitant. Always check before you sign.

The bandwidth works the same way. That data center I described has broadband lines coming into it, just like your server room at work. The cloud vendor pays for that bandwidth, and that bandwidth can handle a certain amount of traffic, measured by the volume of the data sent over the line, both into and out of the data center. The data center pays for bandwidth based on a traffic volume that's actually several percentage points lower than what their actual bandwidth can handle. To make it simple, we'll call this the "safe limit."

If their traffic average for a given time period exceeds the safe limit, they pay extra. When a cloud software vendor charges customers for going over the limits in their software subscription agreement, they are simply passing this cost of exceeded bandwidth through to the customer.

You may find other areas where a cloud vendor will tack on hidden charges, whether it be for additional features such as call waiting, call forwarding and conference calling from phone service providers or another supposed financial imperative similar to bandwidth and storage. Understand that cloud vendors, some more than others, will leverage the fact that you're locked into a contractual agreement for some specific period of time. Depending on their approach to business, they may try to squeeze as much juice out of you, the proverbial lemon, as they can during that time.

On-Premise Vendors

Compare the table below to the one in the Cloud Vendors section.

Cost per user	$2,000
Cost for 40 users	$80,000
Maintenance (20%)	$16,000
First Year Cost	$96,000
Second Year Cost	$16,000
Third Year Cost	$16,000
Fourth Year Cost	$16,000
Total Cost for 4 years	$144,000

I'm using some hypothetical costs here, simply because on-premise software costs aren't as easy to find and aren't really available to the general public on a website somewhere.

The vendor makes the most money on the sale of the software licenses. For the vendor, the ideal situation would be that the customer would buy the new version outright, all over again, when it came out. In that case, the table above would have a $96,000 figure in the third or fourth year, assuming a three year release cycle, making a four year cost of $192,000 rather than $144,000.

It's obvious that that simply wouldn't happen, however, and many companies would simply not upgrade at all, or wait much longer between upgrades. In that scenario, the vendor would simply lose too much from companies waiting on upgrades, and thus the software maintenance plan came into being.

Vendor Losses

What would a vendor would lose if a customer was required to buy each new version outright?

Assuming that customers then adopted a 10 year upgrade cycle rather than the actual three to four:

- **Actual revenue**: If this customer only upgraded once every 10 years and paid outright each time, not paying the 20%

annual maintenance, the vendor would come out roughly $150,000 behind.

- **Customer engagement**: Companies wouldn't need to stay engaged with the vendor if they weren't going to purchase any software again for 10 years. Software companies get a lot of momentum from people anticipating upgrades.

- **Product families upgrade together, encouraging cross selling**: For example, Microsoft's Office 2010 and Sharepoint 2010 are better together. To get the complete functionality of the latter, you need the former. It still works with Office 2007, but the new version is enhanced.

- **Support**: No software company wants to support the version of their software that came out 15 years ago. Minimizing the number of people on older versions of software is in their best interest.

- **Customer loyalty**: When a customer is paying a 20% maintenance fee, that customer is more likely to stay with the vendor's product, taking advantage of the free upgrades, rather than switch to a competitor.

Summary

Make no mistake about it; you will see an increase of cloud computing in the future. The cloud will gain market share. Some applications available on-premise today will be available only as a service in the future, and more applications will be available in the cloud than were ever available on-premise. The question for you to consider is which financial model makes sense for your company right now.

CRM as a Development Platform

Using CRM as a development platform is definitely cutting edge. As far as I'm aware, there are only two vendors that really promote their application like this; Microsoft Dynamics CRM and Salesforce.com. The information in this section is specific to the former, because I can be more specific with that application given my experience working with it. However, the principles are the same for any CRM application that can be customized enough to allow it to act as a platform for custom application development.

The ability to use CRM as a development platform grows out of the need for a CRM solution to be customizable to meet the wide ranging business needs of front offices across the world. Most custom developed business applications utilize a relational database for storage and a web front end for the user interface. Most of them need to implement a set of security and user authentication policies, and many need to be integrated with other applications in the business. A CRM application also shares these characteristics.

As CRM technology has progressed, the extensibility of the CRM application has actually made it an attractive platform for developing custom applications. This section will explore some of the details.

Development Definitions

Extensibility

The attribute of being able to be extended. In the language of computer software, extensibility refers to the ability to customize a program to add, change, or possibly remove features and functionality.

Line of Business Apps

Applications that are used to manage the operations of certain parts of a business. In this chapter, this phrase is abbreviated "LoB apps."

XRM: The Microsoft Terminology

Microsoft has branded the custom developed side of CRM as xRM, in an attempt to communicate the extensibility of the product to manage any other type of data outside of the traditional "Customer" data. For the sake of having a standard lexicon, I'll use that terminology throughout this section.

A solid white paper from Microsoft on xRM which includes actual results from companies who used the xRM framework for LoB app development can be found at the following URL:

crmdynamics.blob.core.windows.net/docs/MS_Dy namics_CRM_Maximize_value_with_xRM.pdf

This concept of xRM isn't a new thing; Microsoft has been promoting this view of Microsoft Dynamics CRM as an agile line of business application platform for several years. However, there's more to the concept than is typically understood at first exposure. I want to outline a few of the key principles of xRM here in this section.

Traditional LoB App Development

1. Business identifies a need.

2. The need is validated.

3. Requirements are gathered and validated.

4. Existing systems are evaluated. If none can meet the requirements, then;

5. Resources are allocated for development and maintenance of the application.

6. Application is developed.

7. Application is deployed.

8. (More than likely) Business requirements shift and new functionality is required;

    1. This could involve the need to integrate with an existing LoB app, such as ERP

9. New requirements are validated.

10. New requirements are developed.

11. New requirements are deployed.

12. Repeat steps 8 through 11.

The problems with this model

As this process is repeated in various areas of the company, the maintenance overhead grows very quickly, due to some of the following:

1. Upgrades. With the constant change and progress in technology, applications tarnish fairly quickly these days. Upgrading a web application to Silverlight or Flex or HTML 5 or other new web technologies, or incorporating new data access technology; upgrading an application's framework to the next version of .NET or Java; or any other upgrade consideration requires a lot of time and a lot of money.

2. Maintenance. The health of an internally developed application requires constant monitoring.

3. Integration. Inevitably, this new application will need to be integrated with other existing applications (step 8.1 in the process outline above). Not only does this require a significant amount of resources in itself, but it also complicates the two considerations mentioned previously; upgrades and maintenance.

4. Limited Extensibility. Once an application is developed, unless it's specifically designed

to be extensible which is a very serious and resource heavy undertaking, it probably can't be extended much without a lot of rework, including rebuilding the User Interface to match data layer changes or vice-versa, ripping out the integration connections to/from other applications and rebuilding much of it from scratch, etc.

5. Security. A very sticky matter. Who has access, and who doesn't? And how is the security model going to be managed? We should suppose that the security model between applications will differ, especially between applications developed during different time periods. The complexity of managing this would seem to grow constantly.

The Alternative: Rapid Application Development using the xRM Framework

xRM is a new way of looking at custom application development. The CRM application is designed for extensibility. Its database structure is fully extensible, allowing the creation of new entities, attributes, and relationships, including 1:N and N:N relationships. It has a rich set of APIs, including traditional .wsdl and .asmx web services as well as REST interfaces, client side scripting, an extensible event pipeline that allows a programmer to execute custom programming logic on almost any of the application's many messages, and the ability to incorporate custom web applications into its interface. It also has a very extensive work flow model.

Any application requiring a rich relational data layer can benefit from the existing capabilities of the CRM application.

Microsoft Dynamics CRM in particular has strong existing integrations with Microsoft Office, especially Outlook. These existing features are by default built in to any custom LOB app developed using the CRM application as a development platform. Users can interact with your xRM application completely from within Outlook, instead of having two applications open. Part of the integration with Outlook includes the ability to work offline. Simple mobile access is also built in.

Additionally, a CRM application may offer deployment in the cloud, giving developers an easy way to make their application highly available and avoid the maintenance demands it would have required if it were hosted on-premise.

---

xRM Definitions

xRM Framework

The set of extensibility features in the CRM application that allows you and your team to build a custom application inside of the CRM application. The "x" in xRM is meant to indicate that an application can be built to manage any part of a business, i.e. "you name it" Relationship Management.

xRM Application

The application built using the xRM framework. This application is housed within your installed instance of the CRM application.

API

Application Programming Interface. A set of external commands presented by a software program so that developers can interact with it.

.wsdl

Web Service Definition Language. An XML based language that is used for describing the functionality offered by a Web service.

.asmx

An ASP.NET Webservices file. ASP.NET is a web application framework developed by Microsoft to allow programmers to build dynamic web applications and services.

REST

Representational State Transfer. REST architectures consist of clients and servers, for example, the Internet.

How xRM can solve the problems with the traditional LoB app development model

I've matched the numbering here to that in the 'problems' section above.

1. Upgrades. The CRM application is upgraded by the vendor, so the technology powering

your xRM application stays current. If you access CRM via a cloud based subscription, there is very little work to upgrade your instance. If you have an on-premise instance, your upgrade path is documented. Most important, your custom application, as long as it has been developed in supported manners, will upgrade with the CRM application with minimal modifications.

2. Maintenance. By building LoB apps on the xRM framework, you effectively consolidate maintenance tasks. If all custom applications are a part of the same instance of the CRM application, your IT resources only have to maintain one application, although there may be pieces like integrated web applications that also require monitoring. Updates are most likely released on a regular cycle to keep the CRM application healthy.

3. Integration. By housing custom LoB apps in the CRM application, you can probably streamline integration development and maintenance as well. Imagine two custom applications that were required to be integrated in the traditional development model. If both of these applications were developed using the xRM framework, then the integration becomes a simple work flow

process which moves data between tables in Microsoft Dynamics CRM. Integration with external applications, such as an ERP system, can be simplified as well, at the very least reducing the number of instances of integration software required.

4. Limited Extensibility. If you can use the extensibility model of the CRM application to build your application, you can certainly use it to modify or extend it. Of course, proper planning is necessary to minimize rework when making changes to your application, but the xRM platform provides the tools necessary. New entities, attributes, entity relationships, and processes can be added with ease. Modifications to the UI are simple, and can even be accomplished without downtime in a live system, if desired.

5. Security. The CRM security model should be very granular. It allows an IT team to manage the security to their applications in one place with a graphical interface.

Customization and Business Specific Functionality

Have you ever considered getting a CRM application designed specifically for your industry? In the introduction, I mentioned the owner of an IT services company who was trying for the third time to choose a CRM vendor. I wrote that he was on a better track than his first two attempts at implementing CRM, but that he was still unproductively focused on finding the right vendor, without first defining his strategy and the technology that he needed to support it. I'm hopeful that his case, however, will turn out OK, and the reason for my hope is that he ended up licensing a CRM application that had built a solution specifically for his industry; an IT services CRM application.

I'm using his case to introduce this discussion on Customization and Business Specific Functionality because those were actually the two principles most at conflict in his decision. He was impressed with the way the CRM application he eventually chose to license addressed the specific needs of his business. He had spoken to multiple people heading companies like his own who used that application and who were having good experiences. He had even said that there was functionality in this application that he didn't even know he needed, but could see himself needing at some point. This was something he saw as a positive, although to me it seemed a woeful indicator of the absence of a well thought out strategy which should have preceded the vendor search.

However, despite this vendor's understanding of the IT services industry and the extensive feature set they had developed to serve it, the application had the customization capabilities of a pair of slacks. There was very little extensibility built into the product. It could only handle 8 custom fields, and those had to be text fields! Though the product continues to be sold, it's really like a tenth grader at a third grade reading level; it stopped progressing with the rest of the class seven years ago.

So this business owner's quandary was this; he likes the product, he thinks it meets the needs of his business now, but he's not sure that it always will. If his business changes in a way that isn't anticipated by the product development in this vendor's quarterly or yearly releases, he may find himself without a fitting solution once again.

Why We Customize

With CRM, customizing isn't something we do to indulge ourselves. It's not the same as the decision to get the custom rims when you buy that new car, which will still roll with the stock wheels. The applications from the major CRM vendors typically come in what we call a "vanilla" state. They're not vertically focused, and so they have the feature set that the widest vertical and horizontal segments of companies are likely to use. Or, if they do come in vertical specific configurations, the configuration for your vertical may or may be exactly what you need. Many companies don't use all of the features available in a CRM application, but most do need to add functionality to execute their CRM strategy.

To some degree or another, extensibility is a capability of most of the major CRM applications.

In the best case scenario, the owner of the IT services company, had he chosen one of the major applications, would have engaged a partner to help him design and customize the CRM application to fit his business and strategy, assuming he would have developed a clearer strategy during the sale and early implementation process. The features that he saw and needed in the IT services specific application would have been built into his instance of the CRM application. At the end of the process, he would have had a solution that, compared to the vertical solution he did license, was equally or more attuned to his business's particular requirements. And, he would have had the ability to make further adjustments and extensions to the application in the future if his business changed; something very likely in today's dynamic environment. In most situations, this approach may be more expensive and resource intensive, but if it's done right, it has a greater chance for success. A process that's resource intensive with regards to employees has, in actuality, a positive impact on the application's success in the organization, because the effort obtains the buy in of those whose adoption is crucial during the implementation.

The App Store and the Future of Customization

For quite a few years, Salesforce.com has had a great app store called the AppExchange. This early, innovative idea that preceded the iPhone app store allowed 3rd parties to build applications that extended Salesforce.com and sell them through this online marketplace. Very similar to the iPhone app store, a customer can purchase an app and have it install to their instance of Salesforce.com. The app may add functionality specific to a vertical market, integrate Salesforce.com with another application, or extend the Salesforce CRM application in some other way. The customer usually pays a subscription fee for the app, and it would transmit their geographical location to companies in China without their knowledge or permission (just kidding!). Even though the AppExchange came before the App Store, it didn't have that problem, that I know of.

Microsoft has also recently introduced their own app store, called the Dynamics Marketplace, which has apps that extend Microsoft Dynamics CRM. Microsoft actually has plans to build an app store for many of its product lines, including the Dynamics ERP products and Azure, their platform as a service offering. One can expect this way of extending CRM applications to become general, at least among the large vendors.

This will fundamentally change the way professional services operate in the IT industry, including CRM solution providers. What a solution provider would once have had to build and custom configure for a customer's specific needs, be they industry specific, department specific, or market specific will most likely be available via the app marketplace. Despite the likelihood that a customer will have multiple apps from which to choose for any given piece of desired functionality, the pragmatic reality is that these apps will probably not deliver the same perfect "fit" to a company's requirements that an old fashioned customization project would have.

This leaves two possibilities: the first is that a customer's desire for a perfectly tailored CRM application evaporates as he or she examines the cost savings and ease of downloading a marketplace app (or apps) which come somewhat close. The second is that a solution provider can take the functionality of the marketplace app as a starting point and build additional business specific functionality on top of it. I think that you'll see some customers in both camps.

Integration with the Existing Technology Stack

When evaluating CRM applications, it's important to consider the software applications already at use within your organization.

A CRM application naturally fits into a certain place in this constellation of applications, and companies frequently want it to exchange data with these other programs. I mentioned ERP in the introduction, but there are many other applications to consider as well, such as a content management application, the corporate email system, a marketing automation application, an HR management system, a social media management application, etc. etc. etc.

Consider which applications are already embedded in your organization's work processes. Are there any that could be integrated with CRM in a way that would truly add value to your business? If the answer is yes, then a requirement to add to your CRM evaluation criteria is the ease of integrating with those applications. Is there a CRM application that has an out of the box integration with your application?

This discussion involves variable levels of effort for creating an integration, depending on the type of application you want to talk to CRM.

For example, you may have put Microsoft Office on your list. If you didn't, think about it. Most CRM applications integrate with Office in one way or another, whether it be the ability to export a list of records to an Excel spreadsheet, to do a Word mail merge on CRM records, or to integrate Outlook emails, tasks, appointments and contacts with their counterparts in CRM.

If the people who will use the CRM application are heavy Office users, this integration is crucial, as it can fuel adoption by adding a measure of familiarity to the new work process.

It can also help you avoid a productivity lag that may have occurred had users had to learn to do certain things a different way with unfamiliar tools. Fortunately, this isn't the type of integration that should take a lot of effort. Most of the time it's 'out of the box'. The worst case scenario is that you'll have to buy an inexpensive third party tool that provides the Office integration.

Integration with an ERP application, however, is a different story. A CRM-ERP integration involves pushing data from one database into another on a regular basis. Most of the time, this will require a third piece of software specifically built for this purpose. Either application may require updates to its database to be done through its APIs, meaning that the integration software has to be a specialized tool that can talk to the APIs in both systems.

Despite the inherent challenges, many businesses find a great deal of value in integrating applications. It's certainly something you should consider when evaluating a CRM application. Determine whether a viable option exists to integrate the CRM application with the applications you already have.

Conclusion

This list may seem lengthy, but it's always better to know the full extent of a decision's possible impact. Your relationship with the vendor is hopefully going to last for a long time, so take the time to understand the vendor's revenue model and how they plan to make money from your relationship. This consideration is as important as the specific functionality we discussed in this chapter. Perhaps not all of this functionality pertains to you, but now you know it exists and can speak intelligently with the vendors and partners you deal with.

Choosing a CRM Vendor: Conclusion

Now that you've read this book, I hope you feel more equipped for the task of choosing a CRM vendor and moving forward with an implementation. Like all other software, CRM software has come a long way in the past few decades, and many companies are realizing significant benefits from a strong CRM strategy.

Perhaps a short anecdote will provide some closure on the points I've made in the book so far. I've recently been involved in a CRM implementation for a very large manufacturing company. I was impressed with the degree of preparation I saw. They had engaged with the people inside their company who operated in decision making capacities in the parts of the business that would be using CRM. Then, they engaged with vendors directly, as well as implementation partners, to determine the application that could address their requirements the best.

It seems certain that, during this phase of vendor exploration, the requirements continued to fluctuate as discussions about functionality became more specific. They certainly continued to be refined, added and removed during the early stages of the implementation. There were calls between the office where the implementation team worked and an office overseas to debate certain requirements, to interrogate their ability to address the businesses on both sides of the ocean. During this process, we discovered holes in the requirements and worked to redefine the functionality that would properly support the strategies for the business.

This sounds great, doesn't it? It's what I've been talking about throughout the book; understanding the business strategies that need to be supported by the new system, and defining the requirements that take into account both the business processes attendant on the strategy and the functionality available in the CRM application.

However, as it often does, this process also created a complexity that, despite our best efforts, we were unable to resolve into simplicity. One particular part of the business did not understand our desire to deliver the simplest solution possible. The result was a list of nearly two hundred fields that would potentially be filled out during the process of selling a product. Have you ever met a sales person who wanted to fill out two hundred fields?

In this instance, despite our attempts to influence the project towards a more simplistic approach, the customer made the decision to appease this part of the business that demanded the more complex solution. This happens; but at least they made the decision with a full understanding of what the potential implications were. They had the benefit of the implementation partner's experience, and they made a fully informed decision.

So the requirements definition process can get a little bit out of hand. In this, as in the opposite extreme, the role of the partner is essential in keeping things real. The partner can bring perspective with his experience, by introducing things like my 80/20 rule, which states that you should implement functionality to specifically handle or automate the most common 80% of the scenarios you see in the business, and to leave flexibility for the other 20% to be handled manually.

The actual 80/20 split is just a guide; you don't actually have to do the math. The principle, however, is an important one. Over implementation, especially in the first phase of a project can lead to an overly complex system that's too hard to use and too hard to administer. These kinds of projects are usually performed over multiple phases that can span years for larger companies.

Usually, much of the customization created for these over implemented systems is rarely used just a short time after it's created, either because the situations it was meant to address are so rare, or because the business has changed and the custom functionality is no longer relevant. What's the inevitable result? Re-implementation, the same ugly concept we started this book with, although for the opposite reason, which was not enough planning.

So planning is essential, and so is leveraging the expertise of those who have been through this process before. Good luck! And hurry! If you sign now, your business transformation can be complete by the close of the day tomorrow.

Just checking to see if you've been paying attention! Tune out the wild vendor promises, and tune into the strategy of your business. There's a lot to gain by implementing a CRM strategy, but it depends on you having a clear head and realistic expectations.

About the Author

Andrew Schultz has been working in the CRM consulting space since 2007, beginning his career as an implementation consultant at a Microsoft CRM partner.

He is currently a Senior Solution Architect at Celenia Software, an Atlanta, Georgia based company, where he provides subject matter expertise to consulting or software companies engaging in implementation or development projects that utilize Microsoft Dynamics® CRM.

Andrew lives in Houston, Texas with his wife, Camille, and their three children Sydney, Spencer, and Cordelia. His pastimes include working in his church, reading, writing, rooting for BYU lacrosse and football, obligatory Dad activities like lawn mowing and bug killing, and intense, short lived forays into various athletic pursuits like surfing, weight lifting, and running.

Andrew also enjoys connecting with other professionals, so feel free to connect with him in any of the following ways:

Personal site: www.andrewbschultz.com

Blog: andrewbschultz.com/blog

LinkedIn: www.linkedin.com/in/andrewbschultz

Twitter: twitter.com/andrewbschultz

References

1 Lashinsky, Adam. Fortune. "This Time Tom Siebel Guessed Wrong. He never seemed to miss a call on the way up. And he never thought a downturn could last this long." September 16, 2002.

http://money.cnn.com/magazines/fortune/fortune_arc hive/2002/09/16/328587/index.htm

2 Greenbaum, Joshua. ZDNet. "Siebel 2.0: The End of Salesforce.com." May 23, 2007.

http://www.zdnet.com/blog/greenbaum/siebel-20-the-end-of-salesforcecom/117

3 Answers.com. "Siebel Systems."

http://www.answers.com/topic/siebel-systems

Accessed March 8, 2011.

4 Alorie Gilbert. cnet News. "Rivals vie for Siebel's customer spoils." September 27, 2002.

http://news.cnet.com/Rivals-vie-for-Siebels-customer-spoils/2100-1017_3-959878.html

5 Tony Kontzer. Information Week. "Siebel's 2004 Even Stronger Than Expected." January 27, 2005.

http://www.informationweek.com/news/global-cio/showArticle.jhtml?articleID=59100268

6   Jason Stamper. CRM Guru Blog. "Why is Oracle Buying Siebel?" December 19, 2005.

    http://www.crm-guru.com/why-is-oracle-buying-siebel.php

7   Joshua Greenbaum. Datamation. "Tom Siebel Hates Me (And Anyone Else Asking The Tough Questions)." May 14, 2002.

    http://itmanagement.earthweb.com/columns/entad/article.php/11082_1121701_1/Tom-Siebel-Hates-Me-And-Anyone-Else-Asking-The-Tough-Questions.htm

8   Alorie Gilbert. cnet news. "A Second Act for Siebel Systems?" October 4, 2004.

    http://news.cnet.com/A-second-act-for-Siebel-Systems/2100-1012_3-5395891.html

9   Alorie Gilbert. cnet news. "Can Mike Lawrie Make Siebel Better?" October 8, 2004.

    http://news.cnet.com/Can-Mike-Lawrie-make-Siebel-better/2008-1012_3-5402888.html#ixzz1GytqQx9E

10 Datamation. "Oracle to Buy Siebel for $5.85 Billion." September 12, 2005.

    http://itmanagement.earthweb.com/cnews/article.php/3547891/Oracle-to-Buy-Siebel-for-585-Billion.htm

11 Jim Wagner. Datamation. "Siebel: 'We Can Do Better.'" April 19, 2005.

http://itmanagement.earthweb.com/cnews/article.php/3498841/Siebel-We-Can-Do-Better.htm

12 Matt Hines. cnet news. "Siebel expands hosted business despite shortfall." July 8, 2005.

http://news.cnet.com/Siebel-expands-hosted-business-despite-shortfall/2100-1012_3-5780240.html

13 Jason Stamper. CRM Guru Blog. "Why is Oracle Buying Siebel?" December 19, 2005.

http://www.crm-guru.com/why-is-oracle-buying-siebel.php

Accessed March 1, 2011. Website no longer available at date of publication.

14 http://www.cio.com/article/596379/How_to_Escape_the_CRM_Training_Trap?taxonomyId=3005

15 Pricing published by vendors as of Jan. 26, 2011:

Microsoft:http://crm.dynamics.com/en-us/on-demand

Salesforce.com:http://www.salesforce.com/crm/editions-pricing.jsp

Oracle:http://crmondemand.oracle.com/en/about/6055_EN

The Salesforce.com Enterprise edition pricing is used, as that edition has the most comparable functionality to the other vendor products, which only have one version.

16 Economist Debates: Cloud Computing.

http://www.economist.com/debate/days/view/409/